S0-COL-769

LANTERN LANE

BOOK 1

WRITTEN BY
TESSA GREENE

COVER ILLUSTRATION BY
KRISTINA KISTER

© 2024 The Good and the Beautiful, LLC
goodandbeautiful.com

TABLE OF CONTENTS

CHAPTER 1

L etty squinted at the glaring yellow sun, attempting to gauge its position in the sky. It was late afternoon; in only an hour or two, the sun would be setting over the kingdom of Trielle, casting pink and gold beams across the castle and all of the surrounding villages. She glanced down the long lane bustling with people, hoping to see her father in the throng. He had been gone longer than she anticipated, and Letty was growing more concerned by the hour.

She shook her head to clear it of her worries and peeked down into the large wicker basket hanging from her arm. She had one final delivery to make that afternoon for her father's dry goods store, and it was always her favorite. After a quick glance to ensure the road was clear of any wagons or carriages, Letty crossed the street to the cobbler's shop and walked around the back of the quaint stone buildings, stopping momentarily to smell the pink winter roses in the garden. Just beyond the garden, where the cobbler and his family lived, two sets of baby-blue eyes peered expectantly through the window under gingham curtains. As soon as Letty came into view, the eyes vanished from the window, and a moment later, the door flew open. A little boy and girl came racing down the walkway toward her.

"Letty! LETTY!" the children cried in unison, throwing their arms exuberantly around her legs.

Letty laughed sweetly and leaned down to scoop up the little girl, whose hair was tied into swinging blonde pigtails with yellow ribbons. "And how are you today, my little friends?" Letty asked, taking the boy affectionately by the hand.

"Papa made us new shoes!" he said, bouncing and swinging Letty's hand enthusiastically.

"Look!" his sister added, pointing to the leather boots on her dangling feet. "They have flowers on them!" Indeed they did: the sides of each boot were adorned with delicate hand-painted daisies.

"Beautiful, Elsie!" Letty exclaimed before an insistent tug on her hand brought her attention to the little boy.

"Are my shoes beautiful, too?" he asked somberly, as though it were the most important question in all the world. Letty pressed her lips together in a smile, revealing a slight dimple in one cheek, and did her best to suppress a giggle.

"Yes, Liam, your shoes are very beautiful, too." He seemed satisfied with that answer. "Well, let's bring these groceries inside for your mama, shall we?" Letty proposed, shooting a glance at the basket on her arm.

Entering the small kitchen, Letty was greeted by cheery lemon-yellow walls, each plastered with childlike drawings of flowers, ships, mountains, and animals. Red gingham curtains fluttered in the light breeze coming through the open window, and a heavy wooden table sat in the middle of the room, adorned by a vase of winter roses from the family's garden. Letty placed her basket on the table and emptied its contents while Elsie and Liam stood on their tiptoes to watch. Dried beans, oats, cornmeal, jars of applesauce, and packets of yeast were set one by one on the tabletop. Finally, Letty withdrew a round loaf of crusty bread wrapped in an ivory tea towel covered with elegantly embroidered leaves and vines.

As Letty finished unloading her delivery basket, Kiana—Elsie and Liam's mother—entered the room, a cooing infant in each arm.

"Mammy!" Elsie exclaimed, dancing and twirling around the kitchen, her boots tapping and her pigtails bouncing on top of her head. "Letty brought our groce . . . groce . . ." She squinted her eyes, concentrating with all her might on pronouncing the word correctly. "Groc-er-ies," she finally managed to say.

Her mother smiled encouragingly. "Yes, I see that." Kiana had the same golden-blonde hair and blue eyes as her children. She looked tired—Letty could see dark bags beginning to form under the woman's eyes—but that was no surprise. Even though Letty was only fourteen, she knew that taking care of two energetic toddlers and twin infants would be exhausting work for any mother.

As Kiana's eyes scanned the groceries laid out on the table, her smile faltered slightly. "I'm sorry, Letty, but you must have made a mistake. I didn't order any bread."

"Oh," Letty answered cheerfully, "I know. My mother made more than we can eat. You would be doing us a favor to take it; it would only go to waste." This was mostly true. Mama had indeed made more bread than their family had planned to eat, but Letty did not mention that this was intentional. After all, a fresh loaf of bread seemed the least they could do to make life easier for the young mother.

Before Kiana could thank her, Letty's attention was pulled away by another adamant tug on her hand. "Do you want to play wolves with me?" Liam asked. Though his voice was as serious and somber as ever, excitement danced in his pale eyes at the thought of such a game.

"You know I would love to," Letty said, crouching down to look him in the eye, "but I can't today. I have to get ready for my papa to come home from the mountains."

"Your father isn't back yet?" Kiana frowned, suddenly concerned. "I thought he left yesterday morning."

"He did," Letty responded, trying to mask the worry in her voice. "We expected him back last night, but he never arrived. I'm sure he will be home very soon, though." Anxious to change the subject, Letty returned her attention to Liam and Elsie. With a wink to Kiana, she let out a small gasp as her hand flew to her mouth. "Oh my, I nearly forgot!" she cried dramatically.

"What? What?" Liam and Elsie squealed excitedly. They knew what was coming next, and they adored the game Letty always made of it.

With exaggerated motions, Letty pretended to shuffle through her now-empty basket, then patted down the pockets of her dress and apron, muttering loudly. Liam and Elsie looked at each other expectantly, letting out small high-pitched giggles that sounded almost like the chirping of baby birds.

"Ah! Here it is." At last, Letty drew two red licorice ropes from her pocket and placed one into each child's chubby waiting palm.

"Thank you, Letty!" they cheered in unison as they clasped their hands around the treats. They each gave her a peck on the cheek before beginning to nibble on their sweet treasures.

"Yes, thank you, Letty," their mother added with gratitude shining in her eyes.

"Of course." Letty smiled and waved to Liam and Elsie one last time before leaving.

Upon stepping outside, Letty inhaled a deep breath of the crisp late-afternoon air. The words she and Kiana had exchanged about her father replayed in her head. *Of course Papa will be home soon,* she assured herself. Putting a smile on her face, Letty greeted her neighbors cheerily as they walked past, fixed her empty basket into the crook of her arm, and took off racing down Lantern Lane toward home.

CHAPTER 2

D o you see anything, Letty?"
Letty drew her violet shawl more tightly around
her slender shoulders as she leaned out the second-story
window and peered as far down the street as she could.
Flickering orange lanterns lined the cobblestone lane.
Beyond the lights, mountains rose majestically from the
ground, and as her eyes moved upward, Letty could see
the first evening stars beginning to appear like fireflies in
the night sky. All these things were certainly beautiful,
but Letty barely noticed them tonight. She only hoped to
see her father's figure approaching the shop below her.

"No, nothing," Letty said, dejected. For over fifteen
years, her father had journeyed up the mountain nearly
every fortnight to stock the travelers' hut at the peak with
supplies from his dry goods store. In the past, he had
always left before sunrise and returned by sunset the same
day, but this time he had taken much longer: this was the
second consecutive night he had been away from home,
and his family was more than a little worried.

Letty's mother crossed the kitchen to look out the same
window, hoping to see something her daughter hadn't.
After flicking her eyes hopefully up and down the street

for a few moments, she heaved a defeated sigh, pulling the window shutters firmly closed and pacing back to the washbasin on the table. Her husband was nowhere to be seen.

"A storm will be rolling in before long," she murmured, scrubbing vigorously at a plate with her dishrag.

Letty's older brother, Miles, lifted his head from its resting spot on the dinner table. "He didn't take an extra coat, did he?"

"No," their mother replied. "He was supposed to be back before the cold front came."

Miles's square jaw clenched, just as it always did when he was thinking about something that concerned him. Letty came up behind her mother, took the dishrag from her hands, and wrapped her arms tenderly around her mother's shoulders.

"I'm sure he's all right, Mama," Letty assured her, resting her cheek on top of her mother's head. The reality was, she wasn't sure; the mountains could be dangerous, especially if the cold turned to snow, but what good would it do to worry Mama further?

Miles's knuckles rapped slowly and gently against the table, breaking the tense silence in the kitchen. Faster and faster, harder and harder, his knuckles rapped as his jaw continued to clench tighter, until suddenly he shot up from the table with a determined look on his face. "I'm going after him," he said.

"What do you mean, you're going after him?" Mama responded, staring in disbelief. Letty felt the breath leave her lungs for a moment. She was used to her father going up the mountain. He was so familiar with the mountain- side that Letty hardly worried about the danger anymore when he was gone—except for now, of course. But Miles? He had never made that trek without their father, much less with the risk of a snowstorm looming. It was too dangerous.

"I mean that he could be ill or hurt. What will happen to him if he's stranded on that mountain when the storm comes in?"

"No," Letty and her mother replied in unison. Letty was prepared to launch into a long lecture about how Miles shouldn't rush into danger, especially when he didn't know where their father was or what he might need. While she was trying to gather her scattered thoughts, however, Mama took a deep breath and spoke before Letty could.

"No," she repeated, "at least not alone."

Now Miles joined Letty in her shock. "Mama," he said cautiously, being very careful not to sound argumentative. "I'm eighteen years old; you don't need to be so worried. I've gone with Papa twice before, and I can take care of myself."

"Oh, I don't doubt your competency, Miles. I know you can take care of yourself. What I'm worried about is that you may be right: your father could be injured or ill, but you have to realize that going alone is unwise. You don't know what he will need, and you don't know enough about medicines to help if there is a problem. I do. Besides, if he needs to be carried down the mountain, you cannot do it alone. Letty and I need to come, too."

Me? Letty thought, stunned. She had never been on the mountain before, not even with her father; everyone knew she was too scared. And to be there for the first time when there could be a storm? What if she got lost? What if she fell or froze or was caught in a rockslide? The very thought of it started Letty's head reeling.

Miles considered what his mother had said for a moment, then nodded. Clearly he knew she was right.

Deep down in her heart, Letty knew it, too. At that particular moment, however, she was too busy trying to keep her heart from pounding out of her chest to pay attention to anything else it was trying to tell her.

"Miles, go get the extra coats from the attic while I go down to the storage room for healing salve and bandages. Letty, pack the rest of the bread and any other food you can find into the lunch pail."

Immediately, Miles and Mama went about their tasks. Letty, however, had barely heard her mother's instructions; her heartbeat pounded in her ears, and her breathing was quick and shallow. Her legs started to quake beneath her. Afraid she would collapse, Letty stumbled backward, grasping at the air until she finally felt a chair behind her and toppled into it. Anxious thoughts raced like stallions through her head. *No, no, I can't do this. I can't climb the mountain. I'm going to get hurt. Miles is going to get hurt, or Mama. What if Papa is already hurt? But if he is, I can't do anything! I can't help!*

Miles re-entered the room, a large stack of warm wool coats piled in his arms. "Letty, does this coat on top still fit—" He cut himself off when he saw her squeezing her arms around herself, her thin frame trembling like a birch leaf in the breeze. Quickly setting the coats down on the table, he knelt beside her. As he gently folded one of her quivering hands in his own, he tried to catch her eyes. "Letty, what's the matter?"

Letty took a shaky breath. The lump in her throat kept her from answering immediately, so Miles continued. "Papa will be fine. We'll find him and bring him back. It will be all right."

Letty shook her head slowly, and tears began to fill her eyes. Why couldn't she be more like Miles? He was so brave. All he was thinking about was their father and how to help him. How could Letty be so cowardly, worrying about herself?

"That's not it," Letty said, her voice quivering. She avoided Miles's gaze as she spoke, fixating instead on a spot on the floor next to her. "I mean, of course, that's part of it . . . it's just that . . . m-maybe it would be best if only you and Mama go." She began to speak more quickly, rattling off the only excuse she could think of as it popped into her head. "After all, we can't leave the shop unattended. What if someone needs something? I should stay back and run the shop, just in case. Besides, it's not as though I'll be much help if I go."

Miles released Letty's hand and stood. He crossed his muscled arms as his thick eyebrows knitted together. "The shop will be fine for one day, Letty." His voice was not harsh, but it had lost its softness from a few moments before. "People can wait for their groceries, but Papa may not be able to wait for us." In a few long strides, Miles crossed the room and began digging through the cupboards, removing bread, apples, and dried meats and nestling them in the lunch pail. "As for the idea that you won't be much help," he said, turning back toward her and resting his hands on the cabinet tops, "I think you would be surprised. Mama was right. I can't carry Papa down the mountain alone, and you're stronger than Mama is. If he's hurt, I will need your help. If he's sick, Mama will need help treating him, and you can do that better than I can." He paused, casting around for the right words to comfort Letty, but unable to find them, he simply reiterated, "Papa needs you."

"I know," Letty whispered, "but I'm so scared."

Her confession was met by silence. Letty waited for Miles to speak, but the seconds dragged on, feeling more like hours. Finally Letty lifted her head, ready to see disappointment on her brother's face. Instead, she saw that Miles was still leaning against the kitchen cabinets, but his arms were now outstretched to her. Relieved, Letty jumped from her chair and ran to Miles's embrace, letting a small sob escape her throat as she buried her face in his shoulder. Miles wrapped his strong arms around his sister protectively and hugged her while she tried to collect herself.

"It's OK, Letty. You're OK."

Mama appeared at the top of the stairs. When she saw Letty sobbing on Miles's shoulder, she lifted her eyebrows, confused. Miles gently shook his head, quietly indicating that this was a bad time to interrupt; he had things under control. His mother nodded and silently slipped through another door into her bedroom. She knew that Miles was better than anyone at calming Letty.

"I wish I were brave like you are," Letty sniffled after a few moments. Miles squeezed her even tighter, wrapping her as securely and safely in his hug as possible.

"I'm not any braver than you," Miles answered her. "I'm scared, too."

"You are?" Letty pulled away to look at him, finding it difficult to believe that was true.

"Of course I am. I'm scared that we won't find Papa. I'm scared that we will find him and he'll be hurt or that I won't be able to care for him, and I'm scared that one of us will get hurt. But being afraid doesn't mean you're not brave."

"It doesn't?"

"Not the way I see it. Isn't bravery just facing something that scares you straight-on?"

"I guess so." Letty wiped tears from her eyes.

"So you can't really be brave without being afraid first, can you?"

"No. No, I guess not."

"You know, sometimes I think that the bravest thing we can do is take a leap of faith and trust that God will work everything out."

Letty hesitated. What Miles said made sense, but she knew that if she agreed, she would have to try to be brave. Was she ready for that? She still wasn't sure.

"Look, Letty," Miles went on, sensing her hesitation. "Mama and I won't make you do anything. If you truly don't want to come, you can stay home, but I believe you can do this. I think Papa needs you. Ultimately, though, it's your choice."

Letty's heart continued pounding in her chest. Closing her eyes momentarily, she tried to think about things the way Miles did. She was scared, yes. Something could go wrong, true. But if her papa needed her, how could she possibly say no? Besides, if she were to stay behind, she would just worry.

"You're right," she said at last, trying to square her shoulders. "Of course I'll go."

Mama entered the room behind her just at that moment. "Good," she said. "If your father isn't home tonight, we will leave first thing in the morning."

CHAPTER 3

The family was up well before the sun the next morning. After loading themselves with coats, water, bags of medicine, and their lunch pail, the three silently slipped into the early morning. A purplish darkness rested over their little village. Turning their backs toward the looming stone castle with its magnificent presence, Letty, Miles, and Mama faced the mountains. The peaks were dusted with snow; there would be more before long— likely within the next day or two.

Can I really do this? Letty asked herself, trying not to get frantic. She looked to Miles for reassurance. He nodded at her, his expression warm and encouraging as though he had read her thoughts. On Letty's other side, Mama grasped her hand and squeezed it tightly. Letty breathed in deeply and exhaled. Her breath puffed into a cloud in the crisp morning air. Letty gathered the little courage she felt she had, and the three of them strode down the cobblestone street toward the mountains and, hopefully, Papa.

Just over an hour later, the trio reached the base of the mountain. The sky was beginning to brighten, though the sun had not yet risen fully. Miles quickly identified the rough trail they should take, and off they went.

This isn't so bad, Letty thought as they began to hike. The trail was somewhat steep but not terribly so. Letty's long legs easily adapted to the hard-packed dirt trail, though leaves and twigs took every opportunity to snag at her long brown curls. Miles, too, took readily to the path. He was strong; his broad shoulders easily held the weight of the heaviest bags they had brought. An inch or two taller than his sister, Miles had to duck frequently to avoid branches hitting his head or scratching at his face.

Mama, on the other hand, had no need to duck. Even Letty was a full head taller than she was, so the branches passed easily above her. Between her short stature and the tight, plaited bun at the nape of her neck, the leaves and twigs that tangled in her children's hair left her alone. However, the hike was not as simple for her as it was for her children—after all, she was no longer as young and spry as she had been when she was fourteen like her daughter or eighteen like her son. Still, she was strong, and what was more, she was determined to find her husband.

Their journey was nearly silent, with only the occasional interruption to warn one another to avoid a stray rock or a raised tree root in the path. All of them were busy with their own thoughts. Letty, in particular, was doing her best to distract herself from the tiny darts of fear poking at the back of her mind. She did her best to direct her thoughts toward her father, whom she was missing terribly. She imagined him tending his shop, chatting and laughing with customers. She could almost see the cap shoved on top of his tight blond curls and his bright green eyes—just like hers—sparkling with laughter. He would be measuring sacks of flour or sugar, instructing Letty to deliver them to a struggling neighbor—but of course, he would tell her she should not accept payment of any kind. No one in the community could ever go hungry while her father had anything to do about it.

The distraction was mostly effective. Still, Letty couldn't quite shake the nagging anxiety she felt. Horrid images tried to force their way into her head: her father shivering in the snow or with a broken ankle or burning up with fever. Could they find him? Would they be able to get him home safely? What if they couldn't?

Letty squeezed her eyes shut tightly for a moment. *This is not the time,* she chided herself, trying to keep her breathing from getting panicky again. She adjusted her grasp on the lunch pail in her hand, gripping it until her knuckles turned white. The sensation was comforting somehow. She pulled her shawl tighter around her shoulders, hoping to maintain some of her warmth. Even though the sun was rising, a breeze from the north made it difficult to feel its heat.

"Do you want an extra coat, Letty?" Mama asked. Letty nodded. Mama removed a coat from the bundle she carried and held it up for Letty to slip into.

Miles did not seem to notice their delay. He had gone several yards ahead of them. Looking just past him, Letty could see that the trail was about to get much steeper. Her mother saw it, too.

"Perhaps we should rest a few moments before we go on," Mama suggested. She was having difficulty catching her breath, and the grimace on her face told Letty her feet were aching.

Letty nodded. "Miles," she called up to her brother, who was now nearly at the steep part of the trail. He turned at her call. "Mama wants to rest."

Miles nodded and looked to the side. "There are a few boulders just off the path here," he called down to them. "Come up, and we can sit."

Letty and Mama joined Miles among the scraggly trees where the boulders were scattered over the mountainside. Mama took a seat on a low boulder near the path. Letty removed a loaf of bread from her lunch pail and broke off large pieces for her mother and brother while Miles passed around a canteen of water. Letty took a drink, broke off some bread of her own, and found a large rock to climb up on just a few yards away. Dangling her legs over the edge of the rock, Letty sat with her back to the mountain and looked back down toward home.

The castle of Trielle stood out prominently from the surrounding village. Brown and gray stones rose in strong square towers, each lined with battlements. In front of the castle, guards in leather armor marched back and forth, the size of insects from Letty's point of view.

She knew that King Henrick and his niece, Princess Maisy, lived there, but she had hardly ever seen them.

They were much more reclusive than the former king and queen—Princess Maisy's parents—had been before they died. The castle was still mourning their loss, Letty's mother always said. Her mother often told her (usually accompanied by a shake of her head) that if King Henrick had married, she was sure he would not be able to hide away as he did. She would wistfully recount the festivals that used to be so common in Trielle but which King Henrick had canceled completely long ago.

Letty sighed as her eyes wandered from the castle down to the long cobblestone road that led to its strong oak doors. Letty had never seen Lantern Lane from this angle before, but it was very familiar to her. Both sides of the lane were lined with tall, elegant lampposts, one in front of each home or storefront. Lantern Lane was beginning to wake up as the sun rose above the street. Letty could see the milkman making his deliveries, a young boy running down the road with his dog, and a bit further down the lane, three or four men with long poles making their way from lamppost to lamppost, using their poles to extinguish the candle in each lantern.

She imagined that the glowing lantern lights, which illuminated the road from the castle all the way to the edge of the village, would be lovely from the mountain-side in the darkness of night, although she knew that beauty was only a pleasant side effect of the lanterns, not their primary purpose.

The real reason for the lanterns stood south of the village: an ominous dark forest. Just the sight of it made

Letty shudder. The forest, she knew, was dangerous. As a child, she had always been told that the forest was filled with wolves, poisonous plants and berries, and trees so thick and dense they blocked out most of the sunlight. Only the most experienced and prepared adventurers dared to enter, at least on purpose. The problem was that when night fell, it was difficult for travelers from the mountains to tell where the forest ended and the safety of the villages began.

Years before, travelers who dared to journey at night from the neighboring kingdom, Pelorias, often found themselves lost in the forest. Most who entered in this way were never seen again.

The disappearances, of course, upset the people of both Pelorias and Trielle, and they begged the king and queen of Trielle to find some sort of solution. Thus, Lantern Lane was created, with dozens and dozens of beckoning lanterns set aglow each night and extinguished just after sunrise each morning.

"Letty, are you ready?" Miles had come up behind her while she was absorbed in the view.

Letty nodded, shoved the last bit of bread into her mouth, and followed Miles and Mama back to the trail. She looked up the path, which was about to get much steeper than it had been. *This is dangerous. It's too easy to fall! It's too easy to get hurt!* The thoughts rushing into her head made her hesitate. Miles noticed this and locked eyes with her.

"You're going to be OK," he insisted. "Right?"

Letty breathed in deeply, drew herself up to her full height, and nodded emphatically. "Right." She released the breath she had been holding. "Let's go."

CHAPTER 4

They had expected the weather to warm up by noon, but it didn't. In fact, if anything, it got colder. Miles and Mama had now donned extra coats, too. Dark clouds had rolled in and covered the sun almost completely, and Letty and her family looked up at the sky every few minutes, hoping against hope that the day would pass without the snow they were expecting to fall. Hiking the steep mountainside was difficult enough without slush or ice impeding their progress. By early afternoon, however, the breeze that had been whispering over them all morning became harder, sharper, and icier, and the clouds above their heads looked heavier and angrier.

Letty had been trying desperately to suppress her fears all day. She had been proud of herself for the control she had demonstrated, but now, seeing the snowstorm ready to bear down upon them, her shivers were not due exclusively to the cold.

Storm clouds were not the only thing looming above them; tension, too, was thick in the air. Letty could see worry in Mama's eyes. Even Miles seemed to have lost some of the confidence he typically carried. They were a little over halfway up the mountain now, and there had been no sign of Papa.

If the storm is coming, Letty thought, *please let it wait until after we've found Papa.*

Hardly had she finished the thought when she felt a small freezing sensation near the tip of her nose. If she crossed her eyes, Letty could just see it—a snowflake melting against her skin.

Hesitantly, she looked to Miles, who was a few steps ahead of her. He had stopped in his tracks, one hand gently pressed against his cheek. He had felt a snowflake, too, it seemed.

"Maybe this will be a nice light snowfall," Letty offered, though her optimistic statement sounded more like a question.

"Maybe," Miles replied slowly as his eyes darted across the sky.

"Even so, we should hurry," said Mama. Miles and Letty agreed.

Their tentative optimism was short-lived. Only twenty minutes after Letty had felt the first flake, the snow was swirling around them, the wind whipping at their coats. Snowflakes peppered Letty's face like freckles, the cold moisture uncomfortable against her skin. The ground had almost instantly been covered in a film of white, making it difficult for Letty to tell exactly where she was stepping.

"Do you think it's safe to keep going, Miles?" Mama asked, echoing the thoughts in Letty's head.

"I think so," Miles replied, though his voice did not sound fully confident. "Besides, we're more than halfway. It would be pointless to turn around without Papa now."

Worries blew through Letty's head like the wind whistling through the evergreen trees. *This is impossible,* flew one thought. *I can hardly see where I'm going. How are we supposed to climb the rest of this mountain and look out for Papa in these conditions?* Yet Miles had said it was safe, and she wanted to trust her brother. Letty tried to remember what Miles had told her the night before. *The bravest thing I can do is take a leap of faith and trust that God will work it out,* she reminded herself. She nodded resolutely. The snow made her nervous, but Miles was right; they couldn't turn back now without Papa. She was determined to be brave.

As they had feared, the snow impeded their progress significantly. In a certain sense, Letty was glad for the trouble—after all, it was much easier to keep the anxious thoughts out of her head when she had to focus so hard on where to place her feet. As the snow deepened, Letty and Mama began to walk in a close, single-file line behind Miles, who had both the largest feet and the newest, most durable boots. Each time Miles took a step, Letty carefully placed her feet in the holes left by Miles's footprints, keeping the snow from soaking into her boots.

They continued to hike in that formation for some time until, eventually, they came across a large snow-covered mound beside the trail. *It looks almost like a snowman,* Letty thought.

"I think this is the marker that Papa and I always looked for." Miles sounded enthusiastic at the thought. He leaned toward the mound and brushed the snow from its base, revealing three large rocks stacked on top of one another. "We're close now," Miles announced through chattering teeth, turning his head back toward Letty and Mama. "If I remember right, this means we're about three miles from the hut."

This cheered Letty greatly, and her usual optimism began to bubble up inside her. Perhaps Papa would be there waiting for them, safe and sound away from the storm. There would be a blazing fire—oh, how wonderful it would feel to sit by a fire!—and there would be stew simmering in a large pot, ready to warm her through and through. Then she would see that her worries had been for nothing, and everything had turned out right, just as Miles had promised.

Then Miles slipped.

As if time had stopped, Letty watched him try to stand from his crouched position, placing his foot awkwardly on a particularly slick-looking patch of snow as he did. Letty wanted to warn him to move his foot, but it was too late; his foot twisted terribly before flying out from underneath him. Letty's hand flew to her mouth in shock and horror as he fell hard on his back, knocking the breath from his lungs even with the snow to cushion his fall. As he fell, his ankle cracked against the pile of rocks he had been examining just a moment before, and his yell, short but agonized, fell like thunder on her ears.

A strangled noise broke free from Letty's throat—something between a gasp and a scream. She dropped to her knees next to her brother, and her mother knelt next to her.

"Miles! Are you all right?" Mama asked.

"I think it's broken," Miles replied through gritted teeth, cradling his ankle in his hands.

Mama examined his ankle, feeling it tenderly to determine whether Miles was correct about its condition. Letty, meanwhile, remained perfectly still as though her knees had been frozen to the ground beneath her. She wasn't sure what to think, what to do, what to feel.

"It's hard to be certain," Mama said as she completed her examination, "because it's begun to swell. It could just be sore and bruised, or it could be fractured."

Miles groaned, and Letty felt tears prickling in her eyes. How could things have worsened so quickly, right when she was starting to believe that they would find Papa and everything would be all right?

"What do we do?" she breathed.

"I don't think there's anything we can do other than continue," Mama responded. "It's not as though we can just sit here and let the snow pile up around us." As she spoke, the wind picked up, whistling loudly in Letty's ears.

"What? No!" Letty responded. Then, softly, "We should turn back." The wind blew her voice back down the mountain, making Letty sound as small as she felt.

"We can't turn back—"

"Yes, Mama, we have to!" Letty was not yelling, exactly, but the anxiety she felt had edged its way into her voice. "Miles is hurt, and look around us—can you see even ten feet ahead? Unless Papa is sitting in the middle of the trail waiting for us, we're never going to find him in these conditions."

"We have to move one way or another, either forward or back." Mama's voice was calm but firm. "We're close to the hut now, and Papa may still be there along with the supplies he brought from the shop, which will help us take care of Miles."

"But he can't move." The tears that had been pooling in her eyes now spilled over as she looked down at Miles, who was breathing slowly and heavily through clenched teeth, trying to manage the pain.

"Yes, I can," he gasped, squeezing his eyes shut tightly. "I just need help."

"Miles—"

"Letty!" His eyes flew open, and he looked his little sister in the eye. "I need your help."

"Fine," Letty choked out. "Try to sit up."

Slowly, Miles propped himself up on his hands. His mother hoisted the bags Miles had been carrying onto her own shoulders, and Letty slipped her arm underneath his shoulder and around his torso. Miles gasped in pain as he got to his feet, and he leaned heavily onto his sister for support.

The last segment of the journey should have taken them only an hour under normal conditions, but between the snow and Miles's injury, it took over two. Letty's back and shoulders ached from supporting most of her brother's weight, and all three of them were wet and shivering vigorously. Letty's relief was immense when, at last, she saw the hut standing in the distance.

"Mama, look!" Letty cried. "We made it!"

Letty turned her head and looked over her shoulder at Mama, beaming at their success as she did so. Her smile fell, however, when she saw that her mother had stopped in her tracks. "What's the matter?"

"The windows are dark." Mama's voice was heavy with disappointment.

Letty squinted again at the building. After a moment, she saw Mama was right: there was no sign of a fire burning inside, no sign that anyone—including their father—was there.

"Maybe we just can't see properly from here. Come on, let's go look around." Letty grunted, adjusting Miles's weight, and staggered forward once again. She refused to accept that they had come all this way for nothing, not until it was impossible to deny. She tried not to think of what it would mean if Papa really wasn't there.

The moment Mama opened the door, it was abundantly clear that he wasn't waiting through the storm at the hut. The room was ice-cold, scarcely warmer than the weather outside, and the fireplace did not appear to have been used recently. There was no one resting in the cot against the back wall, no one reclining in the sturdy wooden chair by the fireplace, no one eating at the small round table next to it. Letty gently set Miles, who could hardly focus on anything through the pain in his ankle, down in the chair.

She stood in the middle of the room, staring at the fireplace. Letty had thought her papa would be there with a fire already burning—maybe it had only been a foolish fantasy, but she had clung to it. Now she wasn't sure what to do.

"Where are all the supplies?" came a shocked voice from behind Letty. Letty turned around to see her mother in front of the one cabinet in the room. It stood tall and open next to the cot. She walked over to Mama and saw that the shelves in the cabinet were almost completely bare. Two taper candles—one broken—sat askew on the top shelf. A basket of hard biscuits and a small bag of dried meat both sat nearly empty beneath. It seemed to Letty that the stack of firewood next to the cabinet was smaller than it should have been.

The wheels in Letty's head were spinning. Certainly, this couldn't be all there was. Her father should have brought plenty of firewood, candles, meat, biscuits, and other provisions, and yet there was no sign that the hut had been restocked since her father's last trip a fortnight before. Letty's breath caught in her throat, and her heart rate once again accelerated.

The wheels in her head had clicked to a halt. There was only one logical conclusion: "Papa hasn't been here."

CHAPTER 5

I t took them the better part of the day to get down the mountain the morning after they arrived at the hut. None of them truly wanted to leave, each holding onto a secret hope that Papa would still appear any minute. Deep down, though, they knew that if he hadn't arrived yet, he likely wouldn't be arriving anytime soon. Something was terribly wrong, that was clear, but with Miles's injury and so little food left, they realized they had to return home as soon as the storm abated.

They managed to brace Miles's injured ankle well enough to get him safely back down the path—with Letty supporting him, of course—but when they returned to the village, the doctor confirmed that Miles's ankle was indeed fractured.

Miles's injury made it even more difficult for the family to decide what to do with the dry goods store. Normally, Letty's father ran it with occasional help from Letty and Miles, but with no sign of him in sight, Letty, Miles, and Mama had to decide during a very long suppertime conversation whether they would try to keep the shop open in his absence.

Letty and Miles knew that Mama was busy taking care

of the house and cooking for them and their neighbors, so having her in charge of the shop was not a good option. Mama told them that as much as she trusted Letty, she was certain that the shop was too big a responsibility for a fourteen-year-old, and she was worried that Miles wouldn't be able to do it with his injury. Miles was determined, though.

"Someone has to do it, Mama. The whole village relies on us!" he protested.

"And I can help," Letty added. "I can't run the whole store by myself, but I can make deliveries, and I can help Miles move things around."

At last, Mama relented. Letty could see on her face that she knew her children were right. And so, two days after they had returned from the mountain, Letty and Miles stood in their father's store, preparing for evening deliveries.

"Do you need anything else?" Miles asked as he placed a packet of needles and a jar of fruit preserves into Letty's delivery basket atop the counter of the dry goods store.

"That should be everything." Letty again scanned the yellow-tinted stationery in her hand, where she had written all of the shop's orders for the day.

"I really appreciate your help." Miles adjusted the wooden crutches under his arms. "It makes my arms sore enough to move around the store on these things; I can't imagine how hard it would be to run deliveries with them."

"I'm always happy to help. Besides, I enjoy making

deliveries!" Letty grinned and took two red licorice ropes from the large glass jar next to the cash register, tucking them into the pocket of her dress. "I'll be back soon," she said, waving to her brother as she left. When she stood on the front steps, she hesitated, letting her eyes drift down the lane and toward the mountains.

The rest of the villagers on Lantern Lane seemed just as clueless as Letty was about where her father had gone. Everyone Letty spoke to thought that he had simply been making his regular journey to the hut on the mountain. As soon as it was clear that he was missing, however, the men on the street organized search parties to comb over the mountainside. As many as were available had gone immediately, some leaving their wives or older children to run their businesses for a time, and others promising to join the search in the evenings.

As she stood there on the step, Letty looked up at the Lantern Lane Dry Goods sign above her head. Everything felt strange and empty to her without Papa there.

Letty breathed in deeply through her nose and let out a sigh, releasing the tension in her body. It wasn't possible to stop thinking about her father, nor would it feel right to, but she knew that if he could, he would tell her that worrying wouldn't change a thing. He would want her to put on a smile, let herself hope that the search party would find him, and go make her deliveries. So she did just that: she smiled and waved to a mother walking with her baby, adjusted her shawl to lie more securely across her shoulders, and began her route.

Making deliveries was good for Letty. It was good for her to see her neighbors and be hugged by all the concerned mothers of the neighborhood, and it was also good for her to feel helpful. She stopped by the cobbler's shop to say hello to Liam and Elsie and bring them licorice, even though she didn't have a grocery delivery to make there today. As she walked home with her empty basket on her arm, Letty had a genuine smile on her face. Oh, how she loved Lantern Lane and the wonderful people who lived on it.

"Hello, Letty!" a call came from across the street. Turning her head, Letty spotted a young man carrying a tray laden with bread and muffins coming out the doors of the bakery. Bits of flour clung to his deeply tanned arms, and his face had broken into a wide smile that spread to his cocoa-colored eyes when he saw her.

Letty waved enthusiastically back, then darted across the street to him. "Peter! I'm glad to see you," she said as she came closer. Peter set his tray of baked goods on the sales cart next to him and pulled Letty into a quick, tight hug. Peter had been like a second older brother to Letty for most of her life. He had been Miles's best friend from the time they were small, and like Miles, he had always been very protective and caring toward Letty.

"I came by the shop early yesterday morning," he said as he pulled away from the hug, "and Miles told me all about what happened with your father. How have you been holding up?"

"I've been better," Letty admitted, tucking a stray

strand of hair behind her ear, "but I'm all right. I just finished with some deliveries, and that made me feel much better."

"Is there anything I can do to help?" Peter asked.

"I think we'll be OK," Letty responded, "but keep coming to visit Miles. He can't get out much on his crutches, and I'm sure it won't be long before he starts to go mad."

Peter chuckled. "I'm sure you're right. I'll come by and see him, I promise. I'm also going to join the search party tonight, so hopefully we'll find your father before long."

"Thank you so much." Letty glanced up at the sun, which was dropping low in the clear, cold blue sky. "I need to get back to the shop," she said, "but I'll tell Miles you said hello."

"Please, do," Peter responded, handing her a muffin from the sales cart. "And tell your mother that if she needs anything else, my family and I are glad to help."

"I will, thank you!" Letty turned and started back across the lane, biting into the warm blueberry muffin.

"Move out of the road!" a harsh voice came from her right. Letty turned her head sharply to see an ornate black-and-gold carriage being pulled by two majestic, muscular horses headed straight toward her. Letty scurried out of the carriage's path, then stood off to the side of the road, gazing at the carriage as it went by. The elaborate, intertwining gold vines along the edges of the carriage were captivating. A footman in a deep blue velvet vest stood on one of the back corners; across from him stood an armed soldier in thick leather armor. The person riding inside the carriage, though, was by far the most interesting. Her face was slim, and her features dainty. Thick inky-black hair fell in loose waves to her shoulder blades and was adorned by a delicate silver tiara. *This must be the princess's carriage,* Letty realized, stunned. She could not remember the last time she had seen Princess Maisy ride through Lantern Lane.

As the carriage rolled past, its occupant's head turned in Letty's direction, and Letty was surprised to find herself making eye contact with the princess. A light shiver traveled down Letty's spine under Princess Maisy's gaze. Her eyes were piercing, sapphire blue, and coldly condescending, and they narrowed as she looked at Letty. After a moment of eye contact, Princess Maisy lifted her hand, sharply but elegantly.

"Stop!" she commanded. The harsh tone of her voice perfectly matched her icy demeanor.

The driver reined in the horses, whistling to them until they came to a stop. The princess motioned for the confused-looking footman to open the door for her, and then, surprisingly, she climbed down and began to walk toward Letty.

Instinctively, Letty took a few small steps back, shrinking away from the princess's intensity.

"You, girl," Princess Maisy snapped, raising one long finger to point at Letty. "What on earth do you think you're doing?"

Letty's eyes widened as a mixture of surprise, apprehension, and confusion coursed through her. "Are you speaking to me, Your Highness?" she stammered.

"Of course I am speaking to you. You had no right to run off as you did."

"I-I'm sorry, I don't know what you're talking about." Letty looked down at the princess, who was a few inches shorter than she, and felt as though she were in a strange dream. How else could this conversation be happening?

"Don't feign ignorance. It won't do you any favors with me. You have no idea how difficult it has been to manage without a lady-in-waiting the last two days."

Now things were beginning to make sense: clearly, the princess had simply gotten confused, though it was hard to imagine how she could have mistaken a girl she had never met for one of her personal attendants. Surely she would clearly remember the face of someone who waited on her every day. Letty smiled and shook her head gently. "I'm very sorry, but you must have mistaken me for someone else."

Princess Maisy's dark eyebrows knitted together while her face set in a stubborn frown. "You're being impertinent," she said crossly. "You must return to the castle with me at once."

At that moment, Letty felt a hand rest on her shoulder. She looked up to see Peter standing next to her, his face fierce as it always was when he was being protective of Letty.

"Excuse me, Princess," he said politely yet firmly, "but she's right. You must have confused my friend with someone else. I can vouch that she is not the person you're looking for."

Princess Maisy's glare turned to Peter. "And who are you?" she asked him.

"My name is Peter, Your Highness, and Letty here is a friend of mine."

"Mhm." The princess raised her left hand above her shoulder and snapped her fingers, bringing her footman instantly to her side. "My lady-in-waiting is to come back to the castle with me immediately," she demanded.

The footman hesitated. "But Your Highness—"

"Don't argue with me!" the princess glowered, then stormed back to her carriage.

"Well then, miss," the footman said hesitantly, taking Letty by the arm. "I suppose we should be going."

"No, you don't understand!" Letty yanked her arm away from his grasp. "I'm not a lady-in-waiting. I was just on my way back from a grocery delivery for my family's dry goods store. You have to understand." Desperation crept into Letty's voice as she spoke.

Peter stepped in between Letty and the footman, his arms crossed sternly in front of his chest. "What she says is true," he insisted. "She is not a lady-in-waiting, and she will not be coming with you."

The footman shrank away from Peter. "I don't have a choice," he squeaked pathetically. "Princess Maisy gave her orders."

"Her orders are wrong," Peter said, gritting his teeth.

The soldier stepped down from his place at the back of

the carriage and stood across from Peter with his arms crossed as well. He was much larger than Peter, and his armor and wide shoulders made him look incredibly intimidating.

"Take a step back, boy," the soldier ordered.

Nearly everyone on the street was watching intently. Had there been more men around, perhaps they would have come to stand with Peter and defy the soldier, but with most of the men out searching for Letty's father and most of their wives helping tend to their shops, only a few children and a small number of young mothers were nearby. Those who were close enough to hear began murmuring among themselves, and some loudly voiced their support of Letty's claims.

Peter stood his ground, keeping his eyes intensely locked with the soldier's and making it clear that he had no intention of leaving Letty alone.

Letty's heart pounded as she stood behind him, and she found herself feeling deeply conflicted. On the one hand, she knew that the princess was completely wrong, and it wasn't as though Letty wanted to be a lady-in-waiting, especially when the princess seemed so harsh and cold. On the other hand, Princess Maisy also seemed determined, and Letty realized she would not be able to talk her way out of the situation easily. If she obeyed Princess Maisy's orders, it would keep both her and Peter—who she feared would soon get aggressive with the soldier—out of trouble. With clammy, shaking hands, Letty stepped around Peter and faced the soldier and footman herself.

"It's all right, Peter," she murmured. "Go tell Mama and Miles what happened. Bring my basket back to the shop, too." Without looking at Peter, she extended the basket to him. He hesitated a moment. Letty knew him well enough to guess that he was trying to decide whether to continue fighting, but eventually, he seemed to reach the same conclusion she had. He gave in and slowly, somberly removed the basket from her hand.

"I'll tell them," Peter promised, "and believe me, we will figure out how to fix this, and we'll come get you the moment we do."

Letty only nodded in response. The footman once again came and took her gently by the arm, looking nervously at Peter as he did so, and led her to the front of the carriage to sit next to the driver.

The driver flicked the reins, and the horses once again began clopping down Lantern Lane. Letty looked back over her shoulder at the few neighbors who had been watching, most of whom were still staring after her. The only exception was Peter, who had taken off running up the lane to the dry goods store. Letty took a few deep breaths. If anyone could fix this mess, it would be Mama and Miles—and Peter's help wouldn't hurt, either. At that thought, Letty turned forward and watched the castle loom closer and closer.

CHAPTER 6

When she was a child, Letty had often imagined what it would be like to live in the castle. Nearly every day of her life, she had stared at the grand structure and wondered what it must be like inside. Now, standing at the entrance, she realized that her imagination had fallen short.

The ceilings soared high overhead—high enough that Letty had to crane her head far back to see them. An intricate design of leaves and vines, much like the one Letty had seen on the princess's carriage, was carved into the junction between the walls and the ceiling. Below those engravings on the front and back walls, cathedral-style windows allowed the late-afternoon sunlight to stream into the entry. The walls were made of thick gray stone and were hung with delicately stitched tapestries and richly colored oil paintings. Two sets of heavy mahogany doors were set into each wall, leading to what Letty assumed were equally magnificent rooms, and directly ahead, a large staircase led to a second floor that Letty couldn't quite see. She wondered how anyone could live in such grandeur without stopping to admire it every moment.

"Don't just stand there gawking," the princess snapped, jolting Letty out of her thoughts. Princess Maisy thrust her cloak into Letty's arms and haughtily swept past her toward the staircase. "Nothing has changed during your little escapade, so stop staring like you've never seen it before."

"But Princess, I've tried to tell you, I *haven't* seen any of this before." Letty walked briskly to keep close behind her. "I'm no lady-in-waiting. I've never been in the castle in my life."

The princess whirled around to glare down at Letty from the first step.

"First of all," the princess hissed, enunciating her words slowly, "stop calling me 'Princess.' I've told you before, you are to address me as 'Your Highness.' Is that clear enough for you this time?"

"Yes, Pri—Your Highness. Yes, Your Highness."

"Good. Second, I don't know what kind of game you're playing, but you *should* know that I will not tolerate incompetence. So if you somehow developed amnesia since you ran off, you'd better get your memory back quickly. Otherwise, the next few weeks are going to be very unpleasant for you, girl."

With her condescending yet elegant air, the princess turned and marched up the staircase. Letty stood for a moment, searching for any reasonable explanation for why the princess was convinced that she was the runaway lady-in-waiting. How was she supposed to stay in the princess's good graces when she had no idea what she was doing? For a moment, she considered running. After all, Princess Maisy's back was turned. It would be so easy to throw down the princess's cloak and sprint out the door, down Lantern Lane, and back toward her home. Her body tensed as she looked behind her at the doors she had just come through. If she could just get past them—

But she couldn't get past them. She remembered the guards she had seen as she walked in, two or three of them standing stiff, strong, and tall at the castle entrance. For now at least, she would have to resign herself to the duties for which she was being held responsible. If nothing else, though, she knew there was one thing she could clear up right away.

"Letty," she said loudly. Princess Maisy paused halfway up the steps.

"Pardon?"

"You keep calling me 'girl.' My name is Letty."

The princess turned her head to look partially over her shoulder, a smirk on her face. "Did I ask?"

Letty frowned. *Please let Mama come soon,* she prayed. She wasn't sure how long she could handle Princess Maisy's blatant disrespect.

The second floor, as Letty saw when she reached the top of the staircase, was less imposing and much cozier than the first. A wide hallway ran perpendicular to the staircase, and a set of double doors, much like the ones downstairs, stood directly in front of her. She followed the princess down the hallway, absorbing her surround-ings. The walls were lined with portraits of regal-looking people, each with a name plaque underneath. *King Cornelius II*, read the plaque beneath a painting of a bearded man with a stern face. Another plaque announced its portrait as *Queen Lilliana*, who wore a rich indigo gown and an elegant updo. Letty studied the portraits as she walked. She recognized many of the names—kings who had saved Trielle from destruction or benevolent queens of ages past.

The portraits near the end, though, were most familiar to Letty, for her parents and neighbors still talked about their subjects. *King Magnus* and *Queen Estelle*, their plaques declared. They had passed away in a tragic accident when Letty was only an infant. They were wonderful rulers, she had been told—honest, wise, and virtuous, leading their kingdom with admirable poise and grace. Letty's father had admired them very much, and she couldn't help the wave of sadness that accompanied recalling that detail.

Letty was startled at the thought that the princess—with the same dark hair and light blue eyes as she saw in the portraits—was their daughter. It certainly didn't seem that the princess had inherited her parents' virtues. As she watched Princess Maisy walk down the hallway in front of her, however, she felt a pang of sympathy. It must have been very difficult for the princess to lose her parents at such a young age—she would have been only three or four years old when they passed. Letty wondered how it would be to be raised by an uncle as Princess Maisy had been. The princess was seventeen years old now, almost the same age as Miles. Letty knew her brother still needed his parents, and she imagined the princess did, too.

"Girl!" The princess stood in front of a door, tapping her foot impatiently.

Nearly as quickly as it had come, the pang Letty felt subsided. It was difficult to feel sorry for a person for very long when she was so rude.

"Yes, Your Highness?"

The princess rolled her eyes. "Open the door."

Letty rushed forward to pull the door open, fumbling with the princess's cloak still gathered in her arms, and followed the princess into her bedroom. It was larger than most of the homes on Lantern Lane, and Letty had never seen a room decorated as beautifully and lavishly as this one. The bed was heaped with silk pillows, and white muslin curtains streamed from the bedposts. Against the opposite wall rested a wide white armoire. Flowers of every color adorned nearly every surface in the room, some standing in vases, others resting on tables in elegant bouquets tied with ribbon, and still others lining the tops of the vanity and dressing screen.

"Let's test that memory of yours, shall we?" Princess Maisy said, her voice dripping with a sarcastic sweetness. "Right now, it's half past six. What are you supposed to do at half past six?"

Letty was not one to get easily annoyed, but the princess's condescending air and refusal to believe a word she said certainly pushed Letty's patience. Still, she managed to keep her composure and calmly respond,

"I'm afraid I don't remember. Would you like to tell me?"

It was hard to know whether Princess Maisy's hesitation was because she was upset that Letty didn't remember or because she had hoped to embarrass Letty. Either way, she stared at Letty for a moment, her mouth slightly agape, seemingly uncertain how to respond.

"Well, if I *must* remind you—" The princess straightened her spine and made herself look extra prim, as though trying to erase her reaction from a moment before. "It's time to help me dress for supper."

Letty furrowed her eyebrows in confusion, her head tilting ever so slightly to one side. "Dress for supper? Do you mean to say you change dresses just to eat supper?"

"Of course," the princess replied indignantly.

"Why? The dress you have on now is lovely." It was indeed a lovely dress, jade green with softly puffed sleeves.

"Well, because—because—it's simply what's done!" the princess sputtered. "I want my lilac dress. Fetch it from the armoire."

Obediently, Letty opened the armoire doors and stared at the dozens of marvelous gowns hanging there. After a moment, she managed to select the one that Princess Maisy had requested. The process of getting the princess into the dress, however, was a much longer one, as Letty struggled to fasten the long row of tiny silver buttons while being pelted by annoyed, derogatory remarks from Princess Maisy about how slow Letty was.

Finally, Letty fastened the last button. She brushed off

the gown, admiring the puff of the princess's crinoline beneath the lilac fabric.

"I don't remember what comes next, Your Highness," Letty said innocently as she straightened up. "Could you remind me?"

The princess rolled her eyes. "I'm getting quite tired of this charade, girl." There was a sharpness in her voice that made Letty truly believe her, and for a moment, she felt sorry that she was so little help. Then again, she knew that it wasn't her fault; after all, she had no way of knowing the princess's schedule or expectations, and the princess refused to understand that. What was Letty supposed to do under these circumstances?

Princess Maisy begrudgingly explained, "Normally, you would escort me to supper, then eat in the kitchen, but I don't particularly want your company this evening." She crossed the bedroom to the door, then turned and smirked at Letty. "I hope your memory returns to you well enough to find the kitchen." With that, Princess Maisy swept out of the room.

Letty's stomach growled. While the princess's barb had hardly been fair, Letty realized that she had no idea where the kitchen was, and she was beginning to feel very hungry. Only two options presented themselves to Letty. One was that she could stay in the princess's bedroom and hope that when the princess returned, she would feel generous enough to direct Letty to the kitchen. It seemed unlikely, though, and Letty recognized that she would probably miss her meal if she made that decision. Her alternative was to wander the castle and hope to stumble upon the kitchen on her own.

Another rumbling of her stomach confirmed the decision. Letty crept out of the princess's bedroom, closing the door ever so softly behind her. Down the hall she went, making her way slowly to ensure she kept a distance between herself and Princess Maisy. The last thing she wanted was to run into the princess and somehow upset her. She slipped down the stairs, puzzling over where she would most likely find the kitchen. Letty stared at the four sets of double doors that led from the grand entry. *It must be behind one of these doors, right?* Letty thought. She didn't want to get caught poking around somewhere she shouldn't be, but how else was she supposed to find the kitchen?

She selected a door to try—one on her left—tiptoed over, and pulled the handle. The door was even heavier than it looked, and Letty had to gather her strength and yank with all her might before the door finally creaked open just a crack. Letty put her eye next to the opening, peering into the room. It was long and empty, with no decorations on the cold, hard walls. There was, however, a beautiful red-and-gold carpet leading from the doors all the way to a magnificent throne, with a seat made of soft velvet resting on what appeared to be a solid-gold chair. Letty marveled at the sight. *This must be King Henrick's throne room,* she thought. *All of the most important decisions for Trielle are made in this room!*

Suddenly, a loud whisper jolted her out of her

thoughts. "Isla! What are you doing snooping around?"

Letty whipped around, pressing her body against the door to close it. Standing across from her in the grand entry was an older girl, maybe sixteen or seventeen years old, although she was a good deal shorter than Letty. She wore a black maid's dress, and a long strawberry-blonde braid fell down her back.

Letty's eyes darted around the room, wondering if perhaps this maid was talking to someone she hadn't seen. "I-I'm not Isla," Letty whispered back.

The maid's head cocked to the side as she took a few steps closer to Letty, closely examining her face.

"No, you're certainly not, but you're a near mirror image of her." Letty detected a slight accent in the maid's voice, something about the sharpness of her consonants as she spoke.

A moment of awkward silence passed between the two as the maid continued to look over Letty, evidently admiring the physical similarities between her and whoever Isla was. "Well then, Not Isla," the maid finally said, suspiciously but not unkindly, "what are you doing trying to get into the throne room?"

Letty knew she needed to answer the question, but she had a question of her own that she felt needed an immediate explanation. "Was Isla the princess's lady-in-waiting?"

"Yes," the maid replied, "she was new. She was only here for a few days before she left." The maid glanced around the room and over her shoulder as though ensuring no one else could hear her. Her already quiet tone got even softer, and she leaned in toward Letty. "She just couldn't stand Princess Maisy's behavior any longer; that's why she ran off. She told me she was going to get as far away as she could, maybe even go to Alria or Pelorias." Straightening up, she added, "But you still haven't answered my question. I would rather not have to call the guards, so I really do hope you have a good answer."

"Well, I must look very much like this Isla," Letty chuckled, "because the princess seems to think I'm her, just like you did. She must not pay attention as closely as you do, though, because she refuses to believe I'm not."

The maid's forehead wrinkled. "Oh, I see," she breathed. "I expect she hasn't been pleased with you, then, if she thinks you're the one who ran off."

"No, she isn't," Letty agreed. "That's why I peeked into the throne room—Princess Maisy doesn't believe that I've never been here before, so she left me on my own to find the kitchen for supper."

"Oh dear." The maid took Letty by the hand. "I'll show you where it is; I was just on my way there. My name is Jocelyn, by the way."

"That's lovely," Letty said with a smile. "My name is Colette, but everyone calls me Letty."

"That's a lovely name, too." Jocelyn looked Letty in the eye and spoke seriously for a moment. "I want you to know, Letty, that as long as Princess Maisy thinks you are Isla, I'll do everything I can to help you. You are not alone here."

Letty felt a weight lift from her shoulders. How comforting to find someone in this place who cared about her! Gratefully, she followed Jocelyn through the door next to the throne room and down a narrow hallway to the kitchen.

CHAPTER 7

L etty sat at a large round table in one corner of the kitchen next to Jocelyn, a few other castle maids, a stable boy, and several kitchen hands. In front of each was a cooling bowl of pumpkin soup, but no one was paying much attention to the food; they were too engaged in the conversation they were having.

"Breakfast is at eight o'clock each morning, luncheon is at noon, and supper, of course, is at six thirty," Jocelyn explained. After she had introduced Letty to the others and explained the situation she was in, everyone immediately rallied around Letty, offering advice and describing the princess's schedule to her. She wrote each piece of information on the scrap of paper the stable boy had brought her.

"You'll have to wake the princess," a maid with a squeaky voice said. "She never wakes up on time on her own."

"That will be at seven o'clock," Jocelyn added.

"And don't forget, she takes tea in the garden every afternoon," the stable boy said, happy to contribute to the conversation. Before long, Letty had Princess Maisy's full daily agenda written out before her.

Somewhere in the distance, eight clangs from a clock bell announced that suppertime was over.

"You need to get back to Princess Maisy," Jocelyn urged. She collected Letty's empty bowl along with her own and carried them to the washbasin. "Once the princess goes to bed, I'll meet you at the top of the staircase and show you around a bit. Is that all right?"

"More than all right." Letty smiled. "Thank you, Jocelyn." Jocelyn gave Letty's hand an encouraging squeeze before Letty scurried out of the kitchen, up the stairs, and into the princess's chambers.

By the time Princess Maisy returned to her bedroom, Letty had located a small collection of bath oils and set them out on the end table next to the princess's bed. Her eyes scanned the schedule she had written out to make sure she knew what came next. Then she hastily shoved the paper into her pocket as the door began to open.

"Welcome back, Your Highness," Letty said, taking care to sound as cheery as she could. "How was your meal?"

Princess Maisy narrowed her eyes, skepticism written all over her face. "Mediocre," she responded tersely. "The meat was too dry, and the squash was underdone."

Letty was surprised by such a negative response, although she immediately realized that she shouldn't have expected anything else. Any reply she had been planning to give died on her lips. An awkward silence hung in the air between them for a long moment before Letty remembered the oils on the table next to her. "I was about to draw your bath," she said. "Which scent would you like tonight?"

Princess Maisy lifted one eyebrow. "Oh, so now your memory is coming back, is it?"

Letty shrugged. "I guess something reminded me." Instinctively, her hand went to the pocket where she had deposited the schedule.

The princess pursed her lips, almost skeptically. "Rose oil tonight," she murmured. Of course, within a matter of seconds, she had found something new to be displeased with. "And you shouldn't move the oils from room to room. I don't need to see them laid out in front of me."

"Yes, Your Highness." Letty gathered up the bottles, refusing to let the princess see any slip in the cheer on her face or in her voice. "That bit must have slipped my mind."

"Of course it did," Princess Maisy said, her characteristic smirk returning to her face.

Letty drew the bath, poured some rose oil into the water, and hurried back into the princess's bedroom to fetch her nightgown.

"The silk one, girl," Princess Maisy snipped as Letty removed a soft cotton nightgown from one of the drawers adjacent to the armoire. Obediently, Letty exchanged the nightgown in her hands for a light pink silk one in the drawer. She laid it on the small table next to the bathtub and made sure that everything looked just right before calling the princess for her bath.

"You've used entirely too much oil!" came a shout from

the bathroom almost immediately.

Letty sighed. She located the spot where she had written "Eight o'clock bath." *Less bath oil,* she penciled in next to it. Eventually, she would be able to do something up to Princess Maisy's standards; at least, she hoped so.

Once the princess finished her bath, Letty helped her brush out her hair, pulling much too hard, the princess complained; turned down the covers, much too slowly, according to the princess; and fetched the princess's book from a small pile next to the vanity, although she brought the wrong one the first time and had to try again. Finally, after complaining steadily for over an hour, the princess dismissed Letty for the evening.

"Good night, Your Highness!" Letty chirped as she slipped out the door. From her place in bed, Princess Maisy looked up from her book. She stared disdainfully at Letty for a moment, then went back to her reading without a word.

With the door closed firmly behind her, Letty hurried down the hall. Just as she had promised, Jocelyn was waiting at the top of the staircase.

"How was it? Did the schedule help?" Jocelyn asked, twisting her hands together anxiously.

"It was . . . all right," Letty hesitantly responded. "It did help, but the princess still doesn't seem to be happy with my work."

"I'm sure she'll be better soon," Jocelyn said, sounding not very sure at all. "And hopefully a little tour will make you feel better. Are you ready?"

Letty nodded, enthusiastic to explore more of the castle's beauties.

"Great! I can't show you everything tonight, but it will be a start, at least, so you can get where you need to go. And since we're already right here, there's no better place to begin than the library." With a tremendous effort from her small frame, Jocelyn pulled open the library doors, which were almost twice her size. Instantly, Letty saw that the library was vastly different from any other room she had yet seen in the castle. She thought that it must take up nearly half the second story. Unlike the floors of stone or wood throughout the rest of the castle, this room had floors completely covered in soft currant-red carpeting, with matching chairs surrounding a table on one side of the room. Floor-to-ceiling bookshelves lined each wall, filled with the most elegant books Letty had ever seen, and the shelf behind the table was stocked with rolls and rolls of parchment—maps, Letty guessed, based on the bits and pieces she could see along the worn edges. The space on the other side of the room was filled with even more bookshelves standing in uniform rows.

"Oh, wow," Letty breathed, taking it in. Although Letty had never considered herself a particularly avid reader, the library had a calming effect. Maybe it was the quiet or the fact that there were limitless stories and unimaginable amounts of knowledge stored there. Whatever it was, something about that room filled Letty with peace.

"Beautiful, isn't it?" Jocelyn smiled. "Princess Maisy

spends quite a lot of time in here. I guess she agrees that this is one of the best rooms there is."

Letty tried to capture the feeling of the room like village children captured lightning bugs in jars. *I have to remember this feeling,* she thought, *or visit this room when I'm afraid. I don't know that I've ever felt calmer in my life.*

Too soon for Letty's liking, Jocelyn led her out of the library and through the second-floor hallways, pointing out the three guest bedrooms on the other side of the library, as well as another staircase behind the library, with a guard standing post in front.

"That leads to the third floor," Jocelyn whispered. "That's where the treasury and the king's chambers are." The guard's eyes remained fixed on Letty and Jocelyn, and they quickly scampered away from his scowl, making their way around the library and back toward the first floor.

"This is your room," Jocelyn explained as they walked past a room just down the hall from Princess Maisy's. "Since you will be with the princess most of the time, you'll stay near her instead of with the rest of us in the servants' quarters. We'll skip looking in for now, though, since I'm bringing you back here once we're finished."

In the grand entry, Jocelyn explained to Letty what each adjoining room was. There was the king's throne room, as Letty had discovered earlier that day, and the hallway leading to the kitchen that Jocelyn had taken her through, which also led to the servants' quarters. Across from those doors were a magnificently regal ballroom and a dining hall with a long table that Letty guessed must seat at least thirty people.

"You'll see the gardens tomorrow, I assume, with the princess," Jocelyn told her as they finished the tour and once again approached Letty's new bedroom. "And I hope you don't mind your room too much. It's probably not what you expect after seeing the rest of the castle."

"Oh, I'll be all right," Letty said. "Thank you for showing me around. I'm so glad to have a friend."

Letty watched Jocelyn disappear around the corner before she opened the door, just in case Jocelyn was right that it would be disappointing—she didn't want Jocelyn to be worried or upset if there was some kind of problem.

Letty turned the knob slowly, enjoying the sensation of its raised pattern in her palm, and pushed the door open. Immediately, it became clear that Jocelyn needn't have worried that the room wouldn't suit Letty—though it was only about a third of the size of Princess Maisy's chambers, it was cozy, clean, and simple, just as she liked, and all decorated in cream and periwinkle.

Tentatively, Letty tiptoed over to the small wardrobe next to the bed and opened the top drawer. Two cozy blue nightgowns rested in the drawer. Letty hesitated as she ran her hands along their luxurious material. Was it wrong for her to sleep in this room or to wear these nightgowns? She felt like an imposter even though she wasn't trying to be. All she wanted was her old flannel nightgown and her own bed above Papa's shop. And yet . . . she was so tired. Standing there in front of those drawers, Letty felt exhaustion seeping into every part of her body. Perhaps it wouldn't be such a bad thing to sleep in this bed for one night, just until Mama came for her. She slipped one of the nightgowns over her head, splashed her face with water from a pitcher in the corner, and climbed into bed, relishing the softness of the sheets as she slipped in between them.

As she lay in there in her unfamiliar bed in an unfamiliar room in the unfamiliar castle, the events of the day were beginning to truly seep in. As her heart sank, she tried to recall the calm peace of the library, but the feeling did not come easily.

Please, God, Letty silently prayed, her eyes filling with tears, *let Mama come fix things soon. Better yet, bring Papa back to get me. Papa can fix anything.*

With that final thought, Letty gently cried herself to sleep.

CHAPTER 8

Despite Letty's written schedule, the next day did not begin smoothly. Letty had always woken up with the sun, and that pattern was not broken this morning. Her eyes opened as the first rays of sunlight streamed through the window, enveloping the soft tones of the room in a golden glow. Letty rolled over sleepily, forgetting where she was. Her memory came back to her before long, though, and her eyes fluttered open, searching for the clock she had noticed hanging on the wall before bed the night before. Seven thirty-two, the clock read. She jolted upright. She was late to wake the princess!

With a speed she did not know she possessed, Letty pulled one of the few dresses in the wardrobe off its hanger, paying no mind to the fact that the sleeves came too far above her wrists, that it was ever so slightly too tight in the waist, and that it was her least favorite shade of brown. It was clean and within reach, and those things were more important at the moment. After shoving her feet into her boots, she barely kept herself from running down the hall—she assumed running in the castle would be considered inappropriate. Standing in front of the princess's door, she debated whether she should knock or just enter. She decided on both: she quickly rapped on the door, then pushed it open. She put on a voice that was much cheerier than she felt at the moment, hoping that it would cover her frantic feelings.

"Good morning, Your Highness!" Letty trilled. She crossed the bedroom and opened the drapes to fill the room with sunlight. "We're running just a bit behind this morning, so we need to move quickly."

Princess Maisy groaned. She sat up slowly—Letty wondered in frustration whether the princess was being extra slow just to spite her—and squinted at the clock above the armoire.

"Seven thirty-eight?" Princess Maisy shrieked, throwing the covers off. "What is wrong with you? I *have* to be up by seven o'clock. You've thrown the whole morning off schedule!"

Letty felt tears prickling at the back of her eyes. She hadn't meant to do anything wrong, and she didn't really know how she could have prevented what happened, but she had to admit that she had made a mistake. Now the princess was going to hold it against her all day, and she wouldn't be able to do anything right.

"Which dress would you like today, Your Highness?" Letty asked, fighting back her tears as she tried desperately to be helpful and remedy the situation.

"Just get out of my way," Princess Maisy snapped. "You've done enough to ruin the morning already. I don't trust you to pick a gown—especially not when you're dressed like *that.*"

The princess yanked a maroon dress off its hanger. "No buttons or laces on this one," she fumed as she stormed past Letty to her dressing screen. "Nothing for you to spend all morning fumbling with."

Letty stood helpless as the princess berated her, reiterating over and over again how foolish Letty had been and listing all the other ways she was certain Letty would make a mess of the day. Letty felt horrible. She hadn't meant to make the princess so upset.

And yet . . . Somewhere in the back of Letty's mind, the wheels began turning. *If the princess gets upset enough with me, maybe she'll dismiss me, and then I can go home!* The idea hadn't occurred to her before, but she didn't hate it. It would likely be easier than convincing Princess Maisy that she wasn't Isla, the runaway lady-in-waiting. A stab of guilt poked at Letty, but she did her best to justify it away. After all, she wouldn't be unkind or try to hurt the princess, but perhaps if she was just a little less helpful than she could be . . .

"Help me brush my hair, girl," Princess Maisy said. "And be quick about it!"

Letty picked up the brush and began smoothing out the princess's hair obediently—or at least, almost obediently. The princess may have been telling her to hurry, but Letty took her time working the brush through Princess Maisy's thick dark locks.

"Hurry up," the princess snapped. "I'm late enough as it is."

"I'll do my best, Your Highness," Letty answered

sweetly, "but I would hate to brush too hard. I don't want to hurt your head again."

The princess huffed. "You're going to have to find a balance between the two. I know you don't understand the pressures of being a princess, but I have important things to do, and I don't need you ruining anything."

"Sorry, Your Highness."

Letty could see Princess Maisy glowering at her in the vanity mirror. Feeling guilty, Letty did speed up, but only slightly. By the time she had helped Princess Maisy wash her face, finish doing her hair, and take care of all the other small details that were a required part of the princess's morning routine, it was past eight thirty.

"Come," the princess said. Letty was surprised at the command since the princess had been so opposed to having Letty walk with her the night before. Hesitantly, Letty followed the princess, whose posture was rigid and tense, her lovely features frozen in a rather unlovely scowl.

"I hope you know that your tardiness this morning has not been excused. I will be speaking to the head of staff about this."

"I understand," Letty replied, hanging her head. The same pang of guilt came back, reminding Letty that she really had been an inconvenience that morning. But then again, Princess Maisy had very much inconvenienced her by forcing her into the role of lady-in-waiting, so wasn't Letty justified? She obstinately told herself she was and shoved down any feeling that disagreed.

Once Letty and the princess reached the dining hall,

the two parted ways, and Letty rushed to the kitchen, hoping to find breakfast waiting for her and perhaps comfort from some of the castle staff.

The smell of oatmeal and cinnamon greeted Letty as she entered the kitchen. "Where have you been?" Jocelyn asked, springing up from the table.

"It was a rough morning," said Letty, gratefully accepting a steaming bowl of oatmeal from a quiet square-shouldered cook she had met the previous day. "I woke up late."

"Oh no!" Jocelyn groaned. "The clock in your room should chime to wake you up. I'll help you check it this afternoon."

As Letty began eating, Jocelyn remained standing next to her, shifting her weight from one foot to the other and fidgeting with something behind her back.

"Your mother was here last night," Jocelyn finally blurted out.

Letty's hand stopped halfway to her mouth. "She was?"

"Yes. I didn't see her; I only heard about it earlier this morning. When I came in for breakfast, some of the guards were talking about a woman who came to the door last night insisting that she needed to see her daughter and that there had been some kind of mistake."

Letty held her breath as she listened to Jocelyn's retelling.

"I guess they thought she was confused or maybe that it was some trick to get into the castle," Jocelyn continued. "Either way, they wouldn't let her in."

Letty felt her chest deflate like an overwhipped cake. "They just sent her away? They didn't even check to see if she was telling the truth?"

"I'm sorry, Letty."

What now? Letty wondered. Her head was reeling. Suddenly the full implications of her situation sank in. The previous night and even that morning had been frustrating and frightening, of course, but Letty had believed it was only temporary; she had been convinced that Mama would be there very soon. But Mama had come, and nothing had changed. She was still stuck here in the castle, and any minute now, she would have to go back to Princess Maisy and wait to be criticized no matter what she did, even if it was the very best she could do.

Jocelyn took her hands out from behind her back, revealing a piece of paper clutched in her hand. "She did leave you something, though," she offered, extending the paper to Letty.

Gingerly, Letty took the note and held it, hesitant to open it in front of the others in the kitchen.

"If you want to, you could go up to the library and read it before Princess Maisy arrives for her lessons," Jocelyn gently suggested.

Letty took this advice, feeling as though she were floating through a strange dream as she walked to the library. She shut the door behind her, careful not to make too much noise, let herself down into a comfortable-looking chair at the table, and, with trembling fingers, unfolded Mama's note.

It was not a long message, but Letty felt tears pool in her eyes as she saw her mother's looping handwriting sprawled across the page.

My dearest Letty, the note read. *I will be back. Don't panic.* Letty smiled reading that line. Mama knew her so well. She rested her hands on the table in an attempt to stop them from shaking the way Mama seemed to know they would be.

The note continued: *I will try to get in touch with someone who may actually understand this mix-up. In the meantime, Letty, be calm, kind, and brave. Stand up for yourself, say your prayers, and do the very best you can to meet their expectations. I will come for you as soon as I can. All my love, Mama.*

Letty heaved a sigh. So much for her plan from the morning. If Mama said she needed to try her best and be a help to Princess Maisy, then she would.

The door creaked, and in walked Princess Maisy, who rolled her eyes the moment she saw Letty.

"Oh, how wonderful, you're here," she droned. "I certainly hope you're actually ready for the day now, girl."

After glancing once more at the scrap of paper with her mother's words, Letty stood and curtsied. "My name isn't 'girl'; it's Letty," she reminded the princess, empowered by Mama's advice to stand up for herself. Although she knew the princess hadn't expected an answer, she gave one anyway: "And yes, I certainly am ready."

CHAPTER 9

Letty sat patiently through Princess Maisy's lessons all morning, only half paying attention to the history tutor's lesson on the ancient wars between Trielle and its neighboring kingdoms, Pelorias and Alria. From what Letty had been told by the other servants, she was really only expected to sit through Princess Maisy's lessons for two reasons. The first was that King Henrick insisted the lady-in-waiting must be able to help the princess review what she had learned, although the princess herself never asked for review. The second reason was that Princess Maisy refused to sit through lessons without someone waiting on her to fetch anything she might want or need.

As Letty tried to pay attention to the names of the generals who led each kingdom's armies to battle, her eyes wandered around the library, squinting to read the titles of the books on the shelves. She wished she could look at the maps rolled up on the shelf next to her and, tilting her head, she tried to peek into the centers, but with no luck. Perhaps most distracting, though, was the fact that Letty could sense the princess glancing at her from the corner of her eye. Every so often, Letty would catch her, and Princess Maisy always responded by crossing her arms, letting out a little "hmph," and then focusing back on her tutor with an almost disconcerting intensity. Clearly, Letty was not the only one who was ignoring most of what the tutor said.

Finally, after over half an hour of this silent back and forth, Princess Maisy spoke up. "Won't you please go change out of that hideous dress, girl," she sneered, cutting her tutor off mid-sentence. "It's impossible for me to focus on my lessons with that distracting me."

Letty looked down at her dress, finally noticing the details she hadn't had time to see earlier in the morning. She had to admit that the dress was unattractive, especially because her arms and legs were a touch too long for the style, but Letty really didn't think it was as hideous as Princess Maisy made it out to be. She looked to the tutor, hoping to gain an ally, but he simply looked at the ground and shifted uncomfortably in his chair. Letty, it seemed, was on her own.

"My name is Letty, not 'girl,' Your Highness," she said, careful to keep her voice temperate and calm in spite of the princess's insult. "And I know this dress doesn't fit well, but I doubt the others in the wardrobe will be any better. The only one that fits me is the one I wore here yesterday."

"I don't care," Princess Maisy retorted. "I told you to change your dress, so go!"

Letty felt her shoulders begin to tense as the princess became more insistent. Was this a case where she was supposed to do as Princess Maisy said or stand up for herself? After all, the princess's command didn't seem to have a real reason, other than the fact that the princess was already annoyed and looking for a way to make Letty's life difficult. After a rapid-fire debate between the options in her head, Letty finally made a decision.

"I'll go see if I can find a better option," Letty said, "but I'm not sure if there is one. If not, I hope you'll be patient with me."

"Fine," the princess said tightly. "Now go."

Down the hall Letty went, back toward her room and the dresses she supposed were Isla's—they were certainly not her own. She thumbed through the dresses, looking for any with slightly longer skirts or sleeves that the princess would find less insulting, but as she expected, none of them seemed right. *Although,* Letty reasoned, *while I'm here, I might as well change into a better color.* She removed a pale yellow dress from its hanger. It didn't fit her properly, either, but at least the dress itself was prettier. She hoped that Princess Maisy would find it acceptable.

The moment Letty reentered the library, Princess Maisy looked at her and shook her head. "Hardly better. I should have known not to expect more of you, though."

Letty drew in a long breath. She refused to let Princess Maisy get under her skin, but that was much easier said than done. "Your Highness, these dresses aren't mine. They were just left in my wardrobe, so this will have to do for now."

"I don't want to hear nonsensical excuses. Just fix the problem."

"I'll do my best."

"Fine." Princess Maisy turned to her tutor, her back straight as a rod and her hands clasped tightly in her lap. "Are we finished with the lesson?"

"Well, um, no, Your Highness," the tutor stuttered, fidgeting nervously with the collar of his shirt. "We still have twenty minutes left."

The princess slumped into her chair and folded her arms. "Go on, then," she mumbled. Letty returned to her seat, suddenly very aware of the fast-paced beating of her heart from the conflict. She hoped Mama would be proud of her: she thought she had stood up for herself quite well, given the circumstances.

The rest of the lesson passed without incident, as did Princess Maisy's government diplomacy lessons and religion studies. Princess Maisy now paid rapt attention to her instructors and refused to so much as glance in Letty's direction. Letty didn't mind, though; as long as the princess didn't need her, she was free to let her eyes wander the library or to listen in on the lesson's interesting moments. When the last tutor of the morning concluded his lesson, Princess Maisy stood and turned sharply to Letty. Her mouth dropped open as though about to make some rude remark, but after a moment, it snapped shut again. The princess lifted her chin and spun on her heel, then haughtily paced out of the library.

"Bit of a tense relationship between the two of you, eh?" the tutor said, glancing back and forth between Letty and the library door.

"That's one way to put it," Letty responded.

The tutor chuckled. "Well, she may be difficult, but it's good that you're back—she sure was upset to realize you'd run."

Really? Letty thought. *He thinks I'm Isla, too?* She knew she shouldn't be particularly surprised—after all, his attention during the lessons would be focused on the princess, not the lady-in-waiting. But each time Letty was mistaken for Isla, she couldn't help but think that if they ever happened to meet, Isla had better apologize for all the trouble she had caused.

Princess Maisy kept her distance from Letty for the rest of the morning and through the afternoon. After luncheon and more lessons, the two went for a stroll and tea in the gardens. Princess Maisy stayed ten or twenty feet ahead of Letty, still clearly annoyed by Letty's pushback that morning. Letty was very alert to the princess's needs, as Mama had told her to be. She helped the princess with her cloak before they went outside and tried her best to be attentive to anything else she could do to be useful, but she was happy to let Princess Maisy walk ahead as long as the princess wanted. It gave Letty a chance to study the late-autumn blooms in peace. *The princess must love flowers very much to fill her room with them and walk through the gardens every single day,* Letty thought. Many of the flowers were ones she hadn't seen before—long stems topped with pink blossoms that looked like crepe paper, tiny blue flowers with flossy-looking petals, droopy red-gold petals on stems so thin it seemed impossible that they could support the weight. They were much daintier than the hardy flowers that grew naturally around Lantern Lane. Some familiar flowers sprouted in the garden, too. One in particular caught her attention: a winter rosebush right next to the castle wall, much like the one by Liam and Elsie's house. Letty crouched down next to the bush, leaning in to smell the blossoms. She smiled as she imagined Liam and Elsie picking the star-shaped, five-petaled blooms to give her when she came to visit. As the scent of the flowers filled her nose, a small pang in Letty's chest reminded her how very much she missed her little friends. She wondered if anyone would tell them why she wasn't coming to visit anymore and whether they would understand. Letty plucked a blossom from the bush, just like they would, and slipped it into her pocket.

As she stood back up, a small window—hardly more than a slit near the bottom of the wall next to the winter roses—caught her attention. It seemed odd to have a window so close to the ground, but Letty assumed it must lead to a laundry room in the basement and quickly dismissed it.

"Girl! Where are you?" A shout came from somewhere farther into the gardens.

"I'm coming, Your Highness!" Letty yelled back. She turned away from the winter rosebush and jogged in the direction of the princess's voice.

In the center of the garden, Princess Maisy was waiting for Letty at a dainty white table with two lovely little chairs set under the shade of a cherry tree. Next to the table, a cart from the kitchen held a pot of chamomile tea and warm scones with jam and butter. Letty instinctively licked her lips in anticipation.

Princess Maisy cleared her throat loudly, beckoning Letty to come pour her tea. Letty set the food on the table so the princess could help herself as she pleased, poured the princess her tea, then sat in the other chair, prepared to enjoy teatime. She spread a scone with butter and jam and raised it to her mouth.

"Excuse me, girl, don't you have any manners? Everyone knows that you're supposed to wait for your superiors to begin eating first."

"Oh, I'm sorry. I guess I wasn't paying attention." Letty set her scone back down on her plate, glad she had not yet taken a bite. "And again, my name is Letty."

Princess Maisy rolled her eyes. "And again, I don't particularly care. I don't know why you're so insistent on correcting me when clearly I have more important things to worry about than the names of my staff!" She looked Letty up and down. "Especially a silly lady-in-waiting who doesn't take her job seriously."

Letty looked down at the table, blinking rapidly, and willed herself not to cry. "I really am trying, Your Highness. I know I haven't been perfect, and I know you don't believe I'm not a lady-in-waiting, but I want to help you if I can. I'm doing my best." Letty looked up at Princess Maisy's face, trying to gauge her reaction, but the princess only shifted her gaze off to the side. "And I know

I don't have a royal title," Letty continued, "but with all due respect, Your Highness, I'm a person, too, and at the least I deserve to be called by my name."

Letty held her breath as she waited for the princess's response. After sitting for a moment in silence, Princess Maisy picked up the scone from her plate and took a bite, glancing briefly at Letty to indicate that she could do the same.

Letty and the princess drank their tea and ate the rest of their scones in silence. While it was a bit uncomfortable, Letty noted that the princess didn't offer any more critiques; in fact, she didn't even seem to be looking for them.

Once they had finished, Letty began cleaning up the dishes and leftover pastries as Princess Maisy stood to go back inside.

"You don't have to do that," Princess Maisy said, gesturing to the dishes Letty was gathering up. "That's for the kitchen hands to do."

Letty shrugged. "I'll just put the dishes back on the cart to make it a bit easier for them."

"Oh," the princess replied. "Well, I'll be reading in the library. I'll send for you when I need you, girl." The last word was said nearly under her breath, and the edge was gone from her voice. It was almost as though she was testing the weight of the word and wasn't sure if she liked it. With that, Princess Maisy turned and walked back to the castle.

CHAPTER 10

L etty woke to a sharp rapping on her bedroom door. "Letty! Letty, wake up!" An energetic voice came from the other side—Jocelyn's, maybe? Letty looked up at the clock. She'd been napping for less than an hour. Had something happened? She didn't think Princess Maisy should need her just yet.

Letty rubbed the sleep from her eyes and opened the door to see Jocelyn standing there, a grin on her face and her green eyes dancing with excitement.

"What is it?"

"Princess Maisy received a message," Jocelyn said. "The prince of Pelorias is coming to Trielle in two weeks!"

"Really? Why?"

Jocelyn's mouth was agape, as though she was shocked that Letty would even ask such a question. "To court the princess, of course! This obviously means the whole castle is going to be chaos until he arrives, and you'll have to be prepared for Princess Maisy to be extra demanding. But the royal family from Pelorias is magnificent, and who knows, maybe they will use some of the Pelorian customs at the ball."

"Pelorian customs? Like what?" It was difficult for

Letty to keep up as Jocelyn practically skipped down the hall in excitement.

"Like the dances. I lived in Pelorias when I was young, and the dances there are lovely."

Before Letty could ask any more questions, Jocelyn swung the library door open. A large man stood in front of Princess Maisy. He wore fine clothes, and on his belt hung a sword with a bejeweled golden hilt so beautifully crafted that it could have belonged only to King Henrick.

"This is your duty, Maisy," he boomed at the princess. "I expect you to do whatever it takes to make this visit a success!"

Princess Maisy nodded meekly before meeting Letty's eyes over the king's shoulder. Her demeanor changed in an instant; she straightened her spine and forced the intimidated look off her face.

"There you are," she said stiffly.

The king looked over his shoulder at Letty. His thick dark hair was the same shade as the princess's, and his beard was just beginning to develop streaks of gray. He was the same height as Letty but had a stocky build and broad shoulders. Though his eyes were much paler blue than Princess Maisy's, they were just as cold. His face was set in a frown so hard it looked as though it had been carved out of stone.

"This is your lady-in-waiting?" he scoffed, turning back to the princess. "She looks like a scrawny child. But I guess her looks don't matter to her work. Go, you are dismissed," he added with a wave of his hand.

Princess Maisy flew past him and grabbed Letty by the wrist. "Come," she said, pulling Letty down the hallway. "There's work to do, and even though I'd rather not risk any mistakes, I'll need your help."

Letty decided to dismiss the offhand comment about mistakes; after all, she was curious about the prince's visit, and she wanted to see exactly what was going on. She followed Princess Maisy back to her room.

"Grab some paper and a pencil, girl—" Princess Maisy caught herself and paused, but didn't correct herself. "I need you to make a list."

Letty looked around for paper. Maybe in the vanity? She opened the top drawer and was met only by various kinds of makeup she had never seen before.

"Bottom drawer," the princess said. Letty would have sworn she could almost hear Princess Maisy rolling her eyes.

The paper was exactly where Princess Maisy said it would be. Letty perched on the vanity chair and looked at the princess, waiting for instruction.

"First, I need new gowns made," Princess Maisy began, pacing back and forth across her bedroom floor as she spoke. "And the meals will have to be immaculate and as lavish as they can be. Preparations need to be made for the ball, and, of course, the guest rooms will have to be readied for the prince and his family." Letty thought she detected a slight pink blush creeping onto the princess's cheeks as she spoke about the prince. Letty wrote as quickly as she could while the princess listed each item.

"All right," said Letty as she finished writing, "anything else?"

Princess Maisy thought for a moment. "Not yet. I'll have more specifics once things start to get arranged, but let's talk about what I need you to do."

Letty felt her shoulders start to tense as she anticipated the princess's demands.

"I don't know if this is wise, but I don't have time for everything, so you'll be in charge of getting my gowns ready, which means that you'll have to give the seamstress her instructions. Tell her that the gowns must be splendid—if the prince of Pelorias is coming to court me, he must be impressed. The prince and his family will be staying for three days, so I will need three day-wear gowns, two evening gowns, and, obviously, a ball gown. Make sure she knows that this must be the best work she has ever done. I have to win over the prince.

"You will also help prepare the guest rooms for the prince and his family. The other maids will help you. Everything should be deep cleaned and polished and perhaps even redecorated. The prince must feel comfortable, and he can't feel as though he is missing any luxury from home."

In her mind, Letty ran through all that those tasks would require. It didn't sound so bad. "I can do that," Letty promised. "Is there anything else?"

"Oh, of course, there will be," Princess Maisy scoffed. "Hosting visiting royalty is no simple feat, so there will be plenty more for you to do. Let's see if you can handle those two things first, though, before I trust you with more."

Letty nodded and wrote down the instructions for herself on a separate list at the bottom of the paper, then ripped off the bottom half of the sheet of paper.

"I've got to go speak to Madame Blakely to make sure the ball gets planned. I expect that arrangements will be made for my new gowns by the end of the evening." With that, Princess Maisy swept out of the room.

"Well, then," Letty murmured to herself, "I guess it's time to get some dresses made." Princess Maisy had mentioned a seamstress. Letty sat for a moment, wondering where to find her. Eventually, she decided to go down to the kitchen, where she was sure she'd find someone who could help.

The kitchen was bustling with activity. Kitchen hands dashed back and forth between ovens and tables with dishes full of chopped vegetables and other ingredients as they prepared supper. The stable boy she had met the day before, who had helped her with the princess's schedule, perched on the edge of one of the tables. He was playfully grabbing pieces of food and pinches of bread dough from every bowl and tray that passed by him, laughing as the cooks swatted at him good-naturedly. Letty smiled. He seemed kind and fun, and he was younger than most of the people in the castle—maybe eleven or twelve years old, Letty thought. She decided she would talk to him.

"Hello," Letty said as the boy popped a carrot round into his mouth.

He turned and smiled at her. "Hi," he said once he finished chewing. "Letty, right?"

"That's right. I don't think I heard your name yesterday. What is it?"

"I'm Elias," he said.

"Nice to meet you again, Elias," Letty said. "I was wondering if you could help me."

"Sure, with what?"

"Princess Maisy put me in charge of getting her new dresses for the prince's visit, so I need to talk with the seamstress. Do you know where I can find her?"

Elias nodded. "She lives out in the village," he explained, "but I can help you find a footman to go get her."

"Oh," Letty said, "do we have to fetch her, or could I just send a message? Won't she need the materials in her shop?"

Elias shrugged, unconcerned. "I'm with you; I think she should be able to work from her own shop. I guess the princess is picky about the fabrics and things, though, because we have a workroom that the seamstress uses whenever she gets hired. I've heard there are loads of fabric in there."

"I see. Well, in that case, I would love your help."

Elias hopped down off the table. "I think the footmen were out washing the princess's carriage, so we'll go on a little adventure to find them," he said with a grin, leading her out the front doors. He waved to one of the guards as they exited the castle. "Hi there, Clement. Letty and I are just on our way out to the stables. We're on a special assignment from the princess."

The guard that Elias had called Clement smiled. "Sure you are, kid," he said. "Go ahead."

Elias waved his hand for Letty to follow him as he jogged around the side of the castle, through the gardens, and out back to the stable, where three footmen were polishing the princess's carriage.

"Excuse me, sirs," Elias said as he and Letty approached. "We're on a special assignment from the princess. We need to send for the seamstress."

The three footmen exchanged glances. "And who are you?" one of them asked.

Letty watched Elias's shoulders slump a little as though he was disappointed that they did not know him. "I'm Elias," he said, digging his toe into the ground. "I work in the stables."

"I see," the same footman said. "And the princess sent you to run her personal errands?"

"Yes. Well, not exactly. The princess sent her—" he gestured to Letty— "but she needed help."

"I'm Princess Maisy's lady-in-waiting," Letty cut in. The footmen's skepticism made her feel nervous, but Elias was so kind to help her; she had to be nice enough to help him explain.

"You?" said another of the footmen—a younger-looking one who was maybe a bit older than Miles. "No, you're not. Isla is the princess's lady-in-waiting."

Letty's eyebrows shot upwards. "I, uh—well, you're

technically right. It's a bit complicated, but—"

"The princess thinks she's Isla," Elias interrupted eagerly, "and she won't listen to anybody because she's mad about Isla running away, so now Letty is basically replacing Isla." He glanced over at Letty and leaned closer to her. "Right?" he whispered.

"That's right," Letty confirmed.

The three footmen looked at one another again, and then the young-looking one shrugged.

"All right," he said, "so what is this 'special assignment' that you need the seamstress for?"

"The prince is coming from Pelorias, and the princess wants new gowns for the visit. She asked me to arrange things with the seamstress."

"Well, let's harness up the horses, then," he said, tossing his polishing rag to the side.

"You believe that story?" one of the other footmen asked incredulously.

"Sure," he replied. "You know as well as I do that Isla ran away, and I mean, she looks a lot like Isla, doesn't she? I can imagine that the princess wouldn't bother to notice the difference. Plus, we all knew the prince would come courting one of these days, so that part makes sense, too."

"Fine, then, go ahead and hitch up the horses and run your errand for the kids, Jacob," the other footman chuckled.

He and the third footman put away their polish and rags.

"Do you want to grab a couple of the horses from the

80

field for me, kiddo?" the young footman asked Elias. Elias's face lit up. He nodded vigorously and darted off to get the horses.

Letty watched as the footman prepared the harnesses, a thought beginning to whir in her head. She knew she probably shouldn't do this; the sinking feeling of guilt in her chest told her that. After all, hadn't she just committed to listen to Mama's advice and be a good, helpful lady-in-waiting? She had, but it couldn't hurt to try, Letty convinced herself.

"Your name is Jacob?" Letty asked.

"That's me," he responded without looking up from his work.

"Were you friends with Isla?"

This time, Jacob glanced at her. "Yes, we were friends. We lived in the same village growing up."

"Then you know that I'm not really supposed to be here, don't you?"

"Well, sure, I guess. I mean, obviously, you're not who the princess thinks you are, but who knows: maybe you're exactly where you're supposed to be."

Letty paused. That kind of answer made her hesitate to ask her question, and she didn't want to be deterred. Her heart skipped a beat as she drew a breath.

"What if you brought me with you and dropped me off at home on Lantern Lane?" she hesitantly asked.

Jacob leaned up against the carriage. "That isn't going to happen," he said.

"Why not?"

"Because I don't want to get in trouble for helping you run away. I can't afford to lose my job over a poorly executed escape plan."

"Please?" Letty attempted weakly.

"Sorry—Letty, was it?—but until you work things out with the princess, you're not hitching any rides back home with me."

Letty sighed as Elias came back, leading a horse with each hand.

"Fine," Letty muttered under her breath. Elias and Jacob busied themselves hitching the horses to the carriage. Before long, Jacob was sitting atop the driver's perch, ready to ride off.

"I'll be back with the seamstress soon," he promised with a tip of his hat.

Letty watched as he drove off down the road. Part of her wished she was in that carriage, but the other part of her knew that Jacob had been right, just like her mother. She sighed. Knowing it was right didn't keep her heart from sinking, though. She still had to go back into the castle and deal with the princess, a dozen new tasks, and her worries about her father all on her own.

"Thanks again for your help, Elias," Letty said. "What do you say we go back in and get some supper while we wait?"

CHAPTER 11

Making six magnificent gowns in two weeks was an enormous task for a seamstress to take on, even with the addition of a newly hired assistant to help her. While the seamstress pored over bolts upon bolts of fabric in the castle workroom, Letty apologized profusely for giving her so much work on such short notice. The seamstress promised that she understood Letty was only doing her job and that she could handle the workload. She was a professional, after all, and she had worked with Princess Maisy's demands before. Once it was clear that the seamstress and her assistant understood their assignment—including, of course, how spectacular Princess Maisy expected the gowns to be—Letty left them to their work.

By the time Letty climbed up the stairs, it was almost eight o'clock—nearly time to help Princess Maisy get ready for bed.

Letty entered Princess Maisy's room to find her sitting on her bed, writing intensely on a sheet of paper she held in her lap. She didn't look up as Letty entered the room; Letty wasn't even sure the princess knew she had come in. Letty cleared her throat to get Princess Maisy's attention before she spoke.

"The seamstress is here, and she is beginning on your dresses, Your Highness," she said.

"Good," the princess muttered distractedly, still not looking up from her writing.

"She promised her best work," Letty added, "and her plans sounded excellent."

"That's lovely." Princess Maisy didn't change her tone.

Letty rocked back on her heels for a moment, waiting for the princess to make any real acknowledgment of what she had said. After waiting for a few seconds, Letty asked, "Are you ready for your bath, Your Highness?"

Princess Maisy threw down her pencil with a huff, finally looking up at Letty. "Can't you see that I'm busy?" she snapped. "I need you to do your job so I can make plans for the prince's arrival. You know what you're supposed to do, so don't bother asking me about it."

Letty was taken aback by Princess Maisy's harsh response. "I just . . . I just didn't want to interrupt if you weren't ready—"

"Well, now you have interrupted."

Letty wondered what had happened to the somewhat softened version of Princess Maisy she had seen that afternoon, who was not quite kind or gentle, but not nearly as harsh or impatient as she had been before, or as she was being now.

"That wasn't what I meant to do. I'm sorry," Letty said. "I'll go start your bath now. Would you like rose oil again tonight?"

"Peppermint," the princess said, rubbing her temple as

she looked back at the paper in her lap. "I'm getting a headache."

Letty filled the tub with hot water, added less oil than she had before, and followed the rest of the routine from the previous night. She tried not to be upset with the princess, but it seemed so frivolous to panic over dresses and balls while Letty was worrying about her missing father and being separated from her family! When she finished drawing the bath, she paused a moment to take a deep breath before she walked out to see Princess Maisy with her head now fully resting in her hands, gently massaging her forehead.

"How's your head, Your Highness?" Letty asked softly.

"Terrible," Princess Maisy groaned. "Is my bath ready?"

"Yes, with just a little bit of peppermint oil."

"All right." Princess Maisy walked gingerly across the room. No shout came from the washroom this time. Letty wasn't sure whether that meant she had done a better job or whether the princess was simply in too much pain to shout.

Letty arranged the things she knew the princess would need to finish getting ready for bed, then sat and waited. She didn't mean for her eyes to wander over to the princess's paper; it was none of Letty's business what she was writing, even if it did seem to be causing her stress. Without trying, though, Letty could see the words *Preparations for the Prince* written across the top of the page with a long list of tasks written underneath.

No wonder she's getting a headache, Letty thought. She

was sure she would, too, if she was so busy thinking about how to impress a royal suitor. Maybe Princess Maisy's concerns weren't quite as frivolous as Letty had thought.

"Are you feeling any better?" Letty asked as the princess came back into the room, her black hair dripping.

"A little, but not much," Princess Maisy sighed as she dropped into the chair at her vanity. Letty picked up the brush from the vanity and began running it through the princess's hair. She was careful not to pull too hard on the tangles, which she knew would only hurt the princess's head more.

"If I may ask," Letty started tentatively, "do you know why you have such a terrible headache?"

"Stress, I would imagine," Princess Maisy responded, tension clear in her voice.

"Because of the prince?"

"Of course it's because of the prince."

Letty paused a moment, trying to decide whether she should continue talking or drop the topic. *It can't hurt to try to help,* she finally decided.

"I guess I don't understand. Why does it take so much planning for the prince to visit? Everything here is already so beautiful; I can't imagine that the prince would be uncomfortable."

"This isn't just any visit," Princess Maisy scoffed. "The prince is coming courting, which means that if everything goes well, we'll become betrothed and begin making arrangements to be married in a few years. In order for that to happen, though, I have to get him to like me. So it isn't about just making the prince comfortable; it's about impressing him."

"And how do you do that?"

"By dressing beautifully, looking my best, and planning immaculate balls and banquets."

Letty pondered Princess Maisy's response. It didn't sound quite right to her.

"That's how you get a prince to like you? Do those things really impress princes?"

"Of course," Princess Maisy replied, although Letty thought she detected uncertainty in her voice. Then, sarcastically, the princess added, "What brilliant method would you propose?"

"If I were in your shoes, I think I would want to make sure I was being sincere. I would want him to like *me*, not my fancy dresses and banquets."

Princess Maisy pursed her lips, but Letty pressed on.

"And I think a real prince—one who was worth marrying, anyway—would be more impressed by kindness and grace than by fancy things."

"Well, you're not in my shoes, are you? You have no idea what princes like."

"Princes are people, though, aren't they? And don't people like kindness?"

Princess Maisy didn't reply. Letty held her breath, anticipating that the princess would order her to mind her own business or tell her that she didn't care what a silly lady-in-waiting thought. Instead, after a moment, Princess Maisy softly said, "My hair looks fine now. I think I'll finish getting ready for bed by myself tonight. You may go."

Letty was tentative as she set down the hairbrush and tiptoed out of Princess Maisy's room. She couldn't tell whether the princess was angry or not. Before she slipped out, Letty turned to look at Princess Maisy one more time, just to verify she hadn't changed her mind. The princess hadn't moved. She was sitting still, staring ahead at the vanity mirror but not seeming to really see anything.

"Good night, Your Highness," Letty said.

"Mhm," came the princess's reply.

Letty closed the door behind her, trying to puzzle out Princess Maisy's response. Was the princess silently fuming? Or perhaps she was just tired. Letty didn't have much time to contemplate, though, before she saw Jocelyn appear at the top of the stairs with a bundle of clothing under her arm.

"Well! You sure do make life around here more exciting, don't you?"

"Do I?" Letty asked.

"I'd say so. It isn't every day that two young men show up to the stables with a parcel for the lady-in-waiting."

Letty's heart leaped in her chest. She knew exactly who had been there.

"They brought a few of your dresses," Jocelyn went on, "because they knew you didn't have time to pack anything before you came."

"Are they gone already?" Letty took the bundle of

clothing from Jocelyn, but she was hardly interested in it at that moment.

"No, not yet. Elias thought you might appreciate it if he brought them around to your window."

Letty gasped. "Yes! Come on, come on!" Letty grabbed a laughing Jocelyn by the hand, and together they sped down the hall, shoved open the door, and ran to the window. In the darkness, Letty saw a flickering lantern light directly beneath her window, illuminating three faces.

Jocelyn helped Letty push open the window as far as it would go. Though it only swung out about halfway, it was enough for Letty to hear the voices below her as her eyes adjusted to the darker environment.

"There she is!" Elias's voice cut through the night.

"Letty?" And there was Miles's voice. The flickering light showed him leaning heavily on his crutches, with a grinning Peter standing next to him, offering support.

"Miles! Peter! What are you doing here?" Letty called softly.

"We thought we'd bring your dresses," Miles said. "Since, you know, you didn't have a whole lot of time to get ready for your fancy new job." He chuckled. "And good thing we did, too; it doesn't look like the one you're wearing now fits you very well, does it?"

Letty blushed at her brother's teasing and adjusted the sleeves of her dress. "But that's a long way to walk with your ankle. Doesn't it hurt to walk so far on your crutches?"

"Ah, that's where I come in!" Peter said with a laugh. "Much easier to walk while leaning on your best friend than to hobble all the way on crutches."

"Who's that with you, Letty?" Miles asked, gesturing toward Jocelyn standing next to her.

"This is my new friend, Jocelyn," Letty explained. "She's one of the maids here."

"Hello," Jocelyn said with a wave.

"Hi, Jocelyn," said Miles. "Keep an eye on her for me, all right? If I can't be taking care of her, I need someone who can." He smiled like it was a joke, but his voice was solemn.

"I will; don't worry," said Jocelyn.

"Is there any news from the search parties?" Letty asked, bringing an even more serious tone to the conversation.

"Nothing yet," replied Miles. "To be honest, I think some of them are starting to give up."

"Not all of us, though," Peter jumped in. "I'm going back out with a group tomorrow night. We have a few more places to look."

"You'll send word if you find anything, right?" Letty asked.

"Of course," said Miles and Peter in unison.

"It's getting late," Miles added, "but we'll come back sometime soon, all right?"

"Yes, please do!"

With one last wave goodbye, Peter took one of Miles's crutches and draped Miles's arm over his shoulder instead.

Once Miles was comfortably situated, the boys turned and followed Elias back around the front of the castle, and Letty and Jocelyn pulled the window closed against the chilly night air.

Letty didn't like to cry in front of people, especially if they weren't her family members, but as she watched Miles walk away, she couldn't help but let a few tears fall.

"Oh, Letty," Jocelyn said, "are you all right?"

"I'm fine," said Letty, brushing at her cheeks with the back of her hand.

"It's OK for you to be upset. You miss your family, the princess is driving you mad, and you're very young to be dealing with all of this. If you need to cry, I won't judge you." She held her arms out, offering Letty a hug, which Letty gratefully accepted.

"What are the search parties you were talking about?" Jocelyn asked once Letty had calmed herself a bit. "Who are they searching for?"

"They're looking for my father," Letty sniffed.

"Your father? What happened?"

"It's a long story."

"Well, I have time if you'd like to tell it." Jocelyn sat on the edge of the bed, waiting to listen. Letty sat across from her, and for the next hour, she told Jocelyn the whole story. Jocelyn sat captivated. She nodded throughout, asked questions, and offered occasional comfort when Letty began to get choked up. Somehow, she seemed to know exactly what to do and say to make Letty feel comfortable and cared for. By the time Letty was finished telling all she had to tell, it felt like a great weight had been lifted off her shoulders; how comforting it was to have someone to share her struggles with!

"Thank you for listening," Letty concluded her story.

Jocelyn smiled softly. "Of course. Thank you for trusting me enough to tell me. If you ever need to talk about any of this—or anything else, for that matter— please let me know."

It struck Letty as she watched Jocelyn leave the room that Jocelyn had just done what Miles usually would have; he was always the one to listen to her troubles at home. In some ways, Jocelyn felt like an older sister, and maybe that was why Letty found she admired her so much.

As Letty drifted off to sleep, she muttered a quiet prayer, thanking God for sending her a friend to take care of her when her brother couldn't.

CHAPTER 12

Letty was up extra early the next morning thanks to Jocelyn, who had shown her how to use the clock's chimes the night before. She opened her wardrobe, pleased to be greeted by her own clothes hanging there, and put on her favorite outfit, a pine-green dress with white leaves embroidered along the sleeves and neckline. She glanced in the mirror; there was no chance Princess Maisy could get upset with her for ill-fitting clothes today. Letty tied a cream-colored ribbon in her hair as a final touch, working carefully not to let her curls tangle too dreadfully. By the time Letty was prepared for the day, the clock read six forty-five, leaving her fifteen minutes to examine the guest rooms before she had to wake the princess.

Letty tiptoed past Princess Maisy's door as quietly as she could to avoid waking the princess. Past the staircase and around the side of the library she went until she reached the row of guest rooms on the opposite side. She wasn't sure if Princess Maisy had decided which of the guest rooms the prince would stay in, so she poked her head into each.

The three rooms were identical in every way. Each had

thick, old-looking floral curtains covering the windows, with a matching bedspread on a heavy wooden frame. In the opposite corner sat an equally heavy desk and chair, and next to it was a wardrobe made of the same ugly light-colored wood. The rooms felt musty, old, and abandoned. *The princess may have been right about redecorating the rooms,* thought Letty.

She made a mental list of the most important things to do. *The curtains and bedspreads need to be replaced; a good coat of varnish can probably save the desks, wardrobes, and bed frames; and some art on the walls will make it all more welcoming,* she determined.

Letty moved farther into the room to examine the curtains in more detail, sneezing as she inhaled the dust floating in the air. She pulled the curtains back to feel their weight—heavy and durable. Sunlight fluttered across the antiquated furnishings of the room as the curtains parted. What she saw outside the window, though, interested Letty far more than what was streaming in, for if she craned her neck just right, she could see the beginning of a street lined with lanterns on each side. Letty smiled; she could almost see her home from this room. She knew in an instant that she would enjoy her time cleaning and redecorating these guest rooms.

A movement down below caught Letty's eye. She looked away from Lantern Lane and squinted at the purple flash that had grabbed her attention.

A man in a deep purple cloak was climbing over the

wall that separated the castle gardens from the surrounding villages. He was slender and extremely tall, and he scaled the wall like a spider, quickly and easily, then looked around before dropping to the ground inside. Letty's brow furrowed as she watched him start across the gardens toward the castle. She was about to run downstairs and alert the guards when another figure appeared, much nearer to the castle. The second figure was shorter and much stockier than the first, and on his hip was a sword with a golden bejeweled handle. He, too, turned to look around as the cloaked figure approached. Letty's eyes widened as his face became visible to her. It was King Henrick—she recognized him from his lecture to the princess in the library the day before. Letty watched intently as the two men met near the castle wall. She saw the movement of their mouths as they spoke to one another and wished she could hear what they were saying. The figure in the purple cloak said something that he emphasized with large hand gestures. The king nodded energetically in return. *What could he be so excited about?* Letty wondered.

The king and the hooded figure both looked nervously about one last time before they parted. Letty had half a mind to run down and see if she could intercept the king to learn what they had been talking about, but in reality, she knew that was a terrible idea.

Somewhere down the hall, Letty heard a clock chime seven times, startling her away from the window. She decided to push the king and his mysterious visitor from her mind. After all, who was Letty to judge how the king chose to meet with his messengers? She hadn't heard their conversation, so there was really no reason to assume there had been anything wrong with it. She tried to convince herself of this as she bustled back to the princess's bedroom, rapped on the door three times, and entered the room to start the day.

As it turned out, Princess Maisy was much more agreeable when she was woken up at the correct time. She was very compliant as Letty completed the morning routine with her, only nagging at Letty to select a different dress and to pull the laces tighter.

"Your Highness," Letty said once the princess was seated at the vanity. She ran a brush through the princess's hair as she spoke. "I had a few questions about the room for the prince."

"Hmm?" Princess Maisy responded, busy shaping her fingernails with a file she had taken from one of the vanity drawers.

"Is there one room in particular you would like me to prepare for him?"

"I don't care," the princess said. "Someone will use each of them, I assume, so just choose one for the prince and one for his parents. Redecorate those two rooms, and then tidy up the third for a servant to use."

"Would you like me to redecorate the room for the servant, as well? It could certainly use sprucing up."

"That doesn't matter. I'm trying to impress the royals, not their servant, so focus on their rooms. That should be your priority," said the princess.

"Are you sure, Your Highness? All the rooms look quite old."

In the reflection from the mirror, Letty could see Princess Maisy roll her eyes. As Letty continued watching, their eyes met in the mirror. The princess straightened up and cleared her throat.

"Yes, I'm sure. Clean all the rooms, but focus on the rooms for the prince and his parents."

"Regarding redecorating, do you have any specific style you would like for the prince's room?"

Princess Maisy pressed her lips together; it was apparent she was trying as hard as she could not to be rude. "I don't have time to worry about the style. That's why I asked you to do it. I don't have any instructions for you other than to do it well."

"Yes, Your Highness." Letty finished brushing the princess's hair and sent her down to breakfast.

A few hours later as Letty and Princess Maisy waited in the library for the tutor, Princess Maisy began grumbling, just quietly enough that Letty couldn't quite tell whether the princess was speaking to herself or to Letty. "I asked my uncle at supper last night to let me cancel these morning lessons so I can have more time to plan for the prince's arrival, but he absolutely refused. I can't understand it. These lessons are pointless and time-consuming," the princess complained. "He says I need to show the prince that I am intelligent and educated, but I already am; I've taken plenty of lessons.

Why do I need more right now? It couldn't do any damage to skip two weeks."

"Do you have time in the afternoons for planning?" Letty asked, hoping the princess would be pleased if she could help find a solution to the problem.

"Not nearly enough," Princess Maisy said bitterly. "I don't know how I'm supposed to make all the arrangements I need to in only a few hours each day."

"Well, at least you have help! I don't know if I will do everything right, but I will try." At the skeptical look on Princess Maisy's face, Letty added a disclaimer. "And you have everyone else in the castle to help you, too."

Princess Maisy looked at Letty out of the corner of her eye, clearly disdainful—or at least, that was what Letty thought. She was surprised when Princess Maisy replied, "Thank you." The princess sighed. "I still think my uncle is wrong, though."

"But wouldn't a king know better than anyone what would impress a prince? Especially the crown prince of our closest allies?" Letty asked.

Princess Maisy considered this. "I never thought I would sit and take a lecture from my lady-in-waiting. You're impertinent speaking to me that way, girl," she finally said. As she had the day before, she hesitated after saying the word "girl." She didn't bother to apologize, but Letty could tell that the princess was remembering their conversation. She lowered her head and mumbled, so faintly that Letty wasn't even sure she heard correctly, "Of course, you're probably right."

At that moment, the princess's history tutor strolled into the room. "Good morning, ladies. Your Highness, are you ready for your lesson?"

"Of course. Please, let's begin," the princess said.

Based on the princess's frustrations, Letty was surprised to see Princess Maisy fully engaged in her lessons that morning, with only the occasional critical glance in Letty's direction when Letty allowed herself to get too distracted.

When her morning classes ended, Princess Maisy began to rush out of the room, hoping, Letty supposed, to get through luncheon quickly and on to her other tasks. Before she exited, however, Princess Maisy stopped abruptly in the doorway. "Gir—" she started but cut herself off before the word fully left her mouth. She cleared her throat. "I've extended my dance and music lessons for the next few weeks, so we'll be having tea half an hour later than usual." Once she was done speaking, Princess Maisy immediately strode out of the library.

"Yes, Your Highness," Letty replied, even though the princess wasn't there to hear it.

Letty had plans for that afternoon. After helping the tutor pack his things—a service for which he thanked Letty repeatedly—Letty scurried down to the kitchen. She got her meal—a warm, thick slice of bread, some cheese, and a large green apple—as quickly as possible, then sat at a table to wait for Jocelyn. Letty crunched into the apple, her face twisting at the tart sensation as her fingers rapped impatiently against the table, faster and faster with each passing minute. She laughed softly as she realized that she had picked this habit up from Miles; the next time they saw each other, she would have to tell him that he was rubbing off on her.

Finally, after seven minutes that felt like an eternity, Jocelyn walked through the kitchen doors, took her plate from one of the kitchen hands, and joined Letty at her table.

"You look . . . excited? Or worried. I can't tell which," Jocelyn said as she sat across from Letty.

"Both," Letty said. "I'm going to start working on the prince's room after luncheon. I want it to be perfect and show the princess I can do my job well and be helpful."

"That is very sweet, Letty, but don't forget, this isn't *really* your job, so you don't have to spend all your free time doing extra work to please her. The other maids and I will get around to it eventually, I'm sure," said Jocelyn, taking a contented bite from her steaming bread.

"I know," Letty said sheepishly, "but as long as I'm here, I may as well be as helpful as possible, right?" Letty paused, her eyes dropping for a moment. "That's how my mother and father treat people. They would expect that of me, too, and I want to make them proud. When Papa comes back, I want him to be proud of me." That morning as a reminder to be patient, Letty had tucked Mama's letter in her dress pocket alongside the princess's schedule, and now she felt the paper crinkle under her hand as she explained.

"I understand," Jocelyn said. She smiled as she shook

her head. "I hope to be as good as you are one day."

Letty paused, her hand halfway to her mouth. "What do you mean?"

"Oh, you know," Jocelyn went on, completely nonchalant. "You're just good. You're kind, helpful, and loving, even when *certain people* don't deserve it, and you work hard to be cheerful. I try to do all those things, but I'm nowhere near as good at them as you are."

Letty stared at Jocelyn, who continued eating without noticing. Letty had never thought of herself as someone a person might admire, especially someone like Jocelyn, who was older and, in Letty's opinion, much more exceptional than herself: Letty didn't have Jocelyn's ability to read every situation and know how to respond. She didn't know how to comfort people quite the way Jocelyn could, and Jocelyn was easily one of the best listeners she had ever met. And Jocelyn looked up to Letty?

"Thank you," Letty whispered after a moment.

"Of course," Jocelyn smiled, clearly unaware of how powerful her compliment had been.

Just then, the cuckoo clock on the kitchen wall chirped to announce that the time was twelve thirty, halfway through luncheon. Letty sped through the rest of her meal and tidied up her dishes.

"I want to get an early start," she explained.

"Good luck," Jocelyn laughed as Letty, with an unusual level of excitement for someone preparing to clean, bounded off to begin dusting and scrubbing the prince's room.

CHAPTER 13

The rest of the week passed in much the same way: Letty spent each afternoon cleaning the guest rooms—sometimes with help from the maids, other times by herself when the maids were busy elsewhere—while Princess Maisy attended her music and dance lessons. Letty even got one of the footmen to find her a jar of wood varnish, and she had begun to revive the bedroom furniture. Nearly every afternoon as she walked through the gardens for tea, Letty stopped by the winter rosebush and plucked a single flower. It reminded her of Lantern Lane, and that small connection kept her spirits high, especially when the princess was particularly difficult.

Princess Maisy's mood fluctuated on a daily—and sometimes hourly—basis. One moment she was snippy and dissatisfied with everyone and everything; the next she was calm and almost soft. Letty never knew which version of the princess to expect when they met, but she did her best to remain calm and consistent, clinging to her mother's advice and Jocelyn's compliment about her kindness.

Evidence of preparations for the prince's visit was visible all throughout the castle, from the freshly polished chandeliers in the ballroom to the kitchen stocked with the most luxurious ingredients money could buy and the constant stream of activity in the seamstress's workshop.

The seamstress and her assistant had worked from sunup to sundown for four days straight, trying to perfect the princess's gowns until they felt confident enough in their designs to have Princess Maisy try them on. The princess, of course, could not be expected to spend her time in the workshop, so Letty helped carry the unfinished dresses and extra pins for alterations up to Princess Maisy's chambers.

"Your Highness, could you please step up onto this stool?" the seamstress asked. Her assistant gently removed the first dress from its hanger, conscious in her movements of how long it had taken to make and how disastrous any damage would be. It was a midnight-blue velvet with sashes of material crisscrossing elegantly across the bodice. The seamstress helped Princess Maisy into the dress, once again taking particular care to be gentle with it. The hem fell a few inches above the princess's ankle, and her black hair draped softly across the shoulders, gleaming richly against the deep blue.

Princess Maisy twirled back and forth a bit, watching the skirt sway in the mirror in front of her. "Not this one. It's boring."

The seamstress and her assistant looked at one another nervously.

"I mean, look at it. There's nothing special about it, is there?" Princess Maisy continued.

"I think it's lovely, Your Highness. The color looks beautiful on you," Letty chipped in, hoping at the very least to save the seamstress's dignity through her praise if the princess was going to reject the gown.

The princess glared down at Letty; apparently, she was in one of her snippy moods. "The color doesn't make the dress," she said. "The skirt isn't long enough to look properly royal, and the sleeves are too long. Besides, I don't like velvet."

The seamstress cut in, "But I've made you velvet dresses before, and you've never had a problem with—"

"I've made my decision," the princess snapped. "Stop trying to change my mind because I won't do it. Let me see the next dress."

The next dress—a raspberry-colored chiffon with a full skirt and flowy, draping sleeves—did not receive a favorable response, either.

"It's quite nice," the princess mused, "but is it enough for the prince?" She contemplated for a moment. "I don't think it is. Next!"

The seamstress's assistant was biting the inside of her cheek now, trying to hold back tears. Letty's heart sank for her. After all the time she had put into each gown, Princess Maisy was disparaging her work. Letty offered a soft smile, hoping to provide some modicum of comfort. The assistant smiled back, ever so slightly, as she retrieved the third dress. All the while, Princess Maisy was ranting.

"You can't genuinely expect me to wear either of these while meeting the prince. He must get a good first impression, which can't happen if I'm dressed poorly."

"I understand, Your Highness," the seamstress said. "We'll design something for you, don't worry."

"Not just *something*. I need *six* perfect gowns!"

"Of course, Your Highness."

The third of the day-wear gowns—buttercup yellow with a square neckline and puffed sleeves—was not suitable for the princess, either, nor were the evening gowns or the ball gown. Letty could not understand how Princess Maisy could turn down something as beautiful as the ball gown the seamstress presented. The skirt was full and would have pooled on the floor if the princess hadn't been standing on a step stool. The short sleeves were fluttery and lightly ruffled, and exquisite floral appliqués cascaded down the front of the turquoise gown. It fit the princess like a glove, yet she flatly refused to accept it.

"I don't like the fluttery sleeves," the princess complained. "They're too whimsical. I need something that makes me look like a future queen!"

"What if we changed the sleeves? We could make them longer and less fluttery. We can even remove the appliqués if you would like," the seamstress begged, clearly distressed that all her days and nights of work were going to waste.

"No, that won't work. It still isn't what I want."

"Well, what do you want? We want to make you happy, but you didn't give us any specific instructions."

"I don't know!" Princess Maisy shouted. "I don't know what I want. All I know is this isn't perfect, and I can't settle for less than perfection!"

"But Your Highness—"

"No, do you know what? I want you to just get out and fix this. All of you, just get out!"

The seamstress and her assistant hastily packed up, not bothering to be cautious with their gowns anymore. Letty heard the sound of fabric tearing, accompanied by a gasp from the seamstress.

"It's fine," she heard the assistant murmur. "I suppose they're not getting used, anyway."

They cleared out of the room the moment their things were together. Letty considered following them, but she stayed standing exactly where she was.

"I said all of you," Princess Maisy snapped.

"I know," Letty replied.

"So why on earth are you still standing there?"

Letty took a deep breath, and her heart beat faster. The princess was already angry. This was perhaps one of the worst moods Letty had seen her in, but Letty was sure that this was one of those moments when she needed to stand up for herself—and, more importantly, for the seamstress and her assistant whom the princess had mistreated so badly after they had worked so hard.

"Your Highness, I know you're under a lot of pressure, and I'm sure everything feels very overwhelming, but you cannot treat people like that."

Princess Maisy bristled. "I beg your pardon?"

"I mean no disrespect," Letty continued. Her heart thudded against her ribs, and she could feel her hands shaking, yet somehow, simultaneously, she became emboldened as she spoke. "But you have been mistreating everyone around you. You don't seem to have respect for anyone. Not for me, not for any of the other servants in the castle, and certainly not for your seamstress, who has been working day and night on those gowns. You didn't tell her anything about what you wanted. Did you expect that she would read your mind? And do you truly think that yelling at her will help? Trust me, it won't. No one puts in extra effort for someone who constantly criticizes and belittles them. Your Highness, you're better than this."

Princess Maisy stepped slowly off her stool and stalked across the room until she was only a few feet away from Letty. Letty's heart stopped pounding and seemed to drop to the bottom of her stomach. She took a few steps back, immediately regretting speaking up at all.

"How dare you," Princess Maisy spat, angry tears beginning to fill her eyes. "Who are you to tell me I need to change? I am the crown princess of Trielle, and one day, I will be queen. And who are you? A good-for-nothing who runs away from her work, feigns incompetence, and lets her delusional importance bring her to lecture her superiors. You have no right to speak to me this way."

Letty forced herself to meet the princess's glaring, teary eyes. "You just proved my point," she whispered. "You really don't respect anyone."

Princess Maisy rocked back as if Letty had hit her. "Leave," she growled.

It seemed unwise for Letty to disobey this time; she

had pushed enough already. Before she exited the room, however, she paused with her hand on the doorknob.

"I'm not a good-for-nothing," she said softly, "and I never ran away. I know I'm not a princess. I'm just a girl who grew up on Lantern Lane, where we treat people as they should be treated."

"Good for you," came the reply behind her. With that, Letty opened the door and left Princess Maisy to fume in solitude.

CHAPTER 14

Precisely on schedule, Letty knocked on Princess Maisy's door to help her prepare for supper. While the princess was supposed to be planning, Letty had spent the past two hours composing a letter to Mama filled with her frustrations. The writing had been immensely calming.

Perhaps I could have been more tactful, Mama, she wrote. *I wasn't trying to be unkind, but I can see how the princess may have interpreted it that way. I simply didn't know how else to make her understand that something has to change.*

As she scrawled her thoughts across the page, a little voice in the back of her head whispered that perhaps there was still something she was missing. She allowed her eyes to wander back across the pages she had already filled: a page and a half describing the princess's roller coaster of behavior over the past few days, two pages ranting about their argument, and another few paragraphs reflecting on her own behavior and the aggravation she still felt toward the princess.

What part of this have I not thought about? Letty wondered in frustration. The tugging sensation she was beginning to feel in her head did not seem as though it was going to end anytime soon.

After a moment of contemplation, an image came to her mind that she had seen many times since arriving at the castle: Princess Maisy, passing by the portraits of her mother and father. As she imagined this scene, the image she pictured shifted slightly; now it was a four-year-old Princess Maisy staring up at the portraits, feeling lost without her wonderful parents there to guide her. *She really was only a child when they died,* Letty recalled, not for the first time. *How lonely the young princess must have been!* Letty wondered now if perhaps she had dismissed the empathy she felt for the princess's loss too quickly the first time she felt it.

Another scene came to her mind now, from when she had first learned that the prince of Pelorias would be coming to Trielle. She remembered walking into the library and seeing the king—Princess Maisy's uncle, likely the closest thing she had to a father for most of her life—shouting at the princess and then insulting Letty. Was it possible that just as Letty's parents had shown her to be kind, King Henrick had taught Princess Maisy by example that it was acceptable to be cruel? *Maybe,* Letty thought, *it's time that someone showed the princess some grace.*

Letty folded up the paper, wondering if she really needed to send the letter after all. Writing it had helped her sort out her feelings, and now it didn't seem quite fair to share her rant about the princess. No, Princess Maisy's behavior hadn't been right, but Letty knew she wanted to forgive her.

Making her way to Princess Maisy's bedroom, Letty tapped on the door, ready to offer an apology—not for the things she had expressed, but for how she had said them.

"Come in," a weak voice came from the other side of the door. Letty frowned, confused: she wasn't prepared for that tone. She had expected to have to offer her forgiveness while the princess yelled to be left alone.

Letty let the door creak slowly open to see Princess Maisy sitting perfectly still on the edge of her bed. Her hands were folded in her lap, and although Letty could only see the princess in profile, it was clear that her face was red and blotchy, her mouth drawn into a mournful frown.

"Your Highness—" Letty fully intended to apologize for her harshness earlier, but she didn't have time to get the words out.

"I . . . I have something I need to say," Princess Maisy interrupted.

Letty froze. Certainly, this couldn't be good. Letty's shoulders tensed as she braced herself to be berated once again.

"I'm sorry," Princess Maisy finally went on.

Letty wasn't sure she had heard correctly. "Sorry?"

"Very sorry," the princess said softly, staring at the floor. "I thought about what you said, and you're right. I've behaved terribly. I'm so very sorry." Her cheeks flushed bright pink as she spoke, and her words came slowly, as though the admission pained her.

Letty was stunned. "I—perhaps I was too harsh," she stammered, unsure what to do except try to make the apology she had planned.

"No," Princess Maisy assured her, "you weren't. Obviously, I didn't enjoy hearing the things you said, but I needed to."

Princess Maisy smiled at Letty, silently asking for forgiveness.

Letty had already forgiven the princess; before she had even entered the room and heard Princess Maisy's apology, she had already softened. The princess's words only made it easier for her.

"Well, I accept your apology," Letty said, smiling in return. "Even though you're a princess, you are still only human, and humans aren't perfect. What matters is that we keep trying." With the tension completely gone from the room now, Letty cleared her throat. "Now, do you know what dress you'd like to wear to supper?"

The princess's smile widened. Before she could answer Letty's question, however, a knock on the door interrupted their conversation. "Your Highness?" Jocelyn's voice came from the other side.

"Yes?" called the princess.

Jocelyn opened the door just enough to poke her head in. "There's something you must come see."

"Can this wait? I'm trying to dress for supper," said the princess.

"I understand, Your Highness, but it's quite urgent." Her eyes shifted away from the princess. "Letty, you should come, too." Her face looked strained, but Letty couldn't tell whether this was because of sadness, nervousness, or perhaps even excitement.

"All right, then, let's see what this is about," Princess Maisy said. She quickly rubbed her hands over her cheeks and beneath her eyes, eliminating any evidence she had been distressed, then stood and followed Jocelyn while Letty tagged along behind.

Letty wasn't sure what she expected to see, but what she met in the grand entry caught her completely by surprise. A girl—probably near the same age as the princess—stood with a guard on either side of her. She had hair the color of freshly ground cloves, and it fell in loose ringlets down her back. She was thin but not terribly tall, perhaps three inches shorter than Letty. In her face, she was Letty's double, and it struck Letty that unless you looked very closely, it would be easy to mistake them for twins. Her eyes widened as she realized who the girl was.

"What is the meaning of this?" Princess Maisy asked, looking back and forth between Letty and the other girl.

"Your Highness, this is Isla," Letty said, slack-jawed. "Your lady-in-waiting."

"Do I know you?" Isla asked Letty belligerently. Her face twisted into a scowl; she was clearly not pleased to find herself back in the castle she had run from.

A surge of mixed emotions swept through Letty, and

the unexpected feeling of a laugh rose from her chest. "No," she said, doing her best to restrain herself from laughing, crying, or possibly doing both. "You don't, but everyone else seems to think they do."

"Wait just a moment," Princess Maisy said. "Did I . . . does that . . . you . . ." she stammered, unable to complete a sentence. She held one hand up, taking a deep breath to calm herself. After a few seconds, she turned toward Letty. "When you told me you had never been to the castle or performed any of the tasks I asked you to do—you weren't making that up. You were telling the truth."

"Yes," Letty replied.

"Oh. I see."

A confused-looking guard interjected with an explanation. "When your lady-in-waiting ran off, you sent us out to find her, Your Highness," the guard said nervously. "We've been looking ever since. We finally gave up and turned around to come back to the castle when we found this young woman a few villages away. We didn't get word that you had already found your girl . . . or did you?"

"I suppose not," said the princess. "I don't know anymore; I'm confused."

"Your Highness, does that mean you'll send Letty home?" Jocelyn asked, her voice barely above a whisper. Isla turned her glare to Jocelyn, who turned away from the icy look.

"Yes, yes, I guess so," Princess Maisy muttered absently.

"Why bother?" said Isla. "You never liked my work, anyway, so why torture both yourself and me? Just keep her on as your lady-in-waiting and let me find another job."

"Oh, I couldn't—" said Letty, but the princess cut her off.

"No, wait," Princess Maisy said, turning to face Letty. "I actually quite like that idea. I think I would be happier if you stayed than if she did."

Letty's eyebrows shot up. "Really?"

"Yes. I'm sure you understand that sometimes you frustrate me to no end, especially when you decide to push back against me, but in all honesty, it seems like you're usually right. I think it may be good for me."

"So can I leave now?" Isla grumbled.

"Give me a moment," the princess said with a bit of a snap in her voice. She breathed in deeply, getting herself under control, then turned back to Letty, calm again. "I'd like you to stay. I need your help to get ready for the prince's arrival, and I don't want someone else to take over your work. Will you please stay?"

Letty's heart stopped. The whole time she had been in the castle, she had wished that Isla would come back so she would be free to go home. She had been waiting for this exact moment, but now that it was here, it wasn't going at all as she had hoped. Why did the princess want Letty to stay? Letty had thought the princess despised her. And what about Letty's family? Could she leave Mama to take care of the house alone while she worried about her husband? And what about Miles, running the shop by himself with only occasional help from their mother?

What about Papa, out missing who knew where? It wasn't as though Letty could do much to help him at home, but at least she would know more about the search there than she did here.

"You can say no if you want to, Letty," Jocelyn whispered. "Isla signed a contract; you didn't. Now that there's proof that you are not Isla, no one can force you to stay."

"You're taking her side in this, Jocelyn?" Isla asked indignantly. "I thought we were friends."

"I'm not taking sides, Isla. We are friends. But Letty has been punished because you broke your word, and someone should be there to help her. Letting her know she has options is not taking sides."

Jocelyn was right: Letty could say no. Certainly, she should say no, shouldn't she? But Princess Maisy's face was so sincere, and Jocelyn had a wistful look in her eyes, as though she wasn't sure whether to be happy or sad that Letty could now leave. Letty knew she couldn't decide based solely on what other people thought. Yet, as she considered it, Letty realized she didn't want to leave just as she and the princess were starting to reach an understanding. She knew she could be of service as Princess Maisy prepared for the prince, and a part of her very much wanted to try. As Letty made her decision, a feeling of peace settled over her, like a warm hug enveloping her to say that things would turn out just fine.

"All right," Letty said slowly, "I'll stay, but only if you agree to some conditions."

"What conditions?" the princess asked.

"First, if I stay, you can't call me 'girl' anymore. You have to call me Letty."

"I will. I promise."

"Second, I need to be able to leave the castle. I miss Lantern Lane, and I miss my family, so if I stay, I want to be able to go visit my home."

The princess shifted her eyes, a concerned expression crossing her face. "How often will you be gone?"

Letty thought about it for a moment. "As frequently as I want," she said. The princess opened her mouth to protest, but Letty held up one hand and continued. "As long as I do my work. I'll only visit home during my free time when you don't need me." Princess Maisy closed her mouth again, seemingly satisfied. "And third, if you want me to stay—especially if you want my help getting ready for the prince—I want you to try to do things my way."

"What do you mean 'your way'?"

"Remember when I told you that a good prince will appreciate kindness and grace more than fancy things?"

"Yes, I remember."

"If I stay, will you promise to make that more of a priority than the fancy dresses or extravagant balls?" Letty asked.

Princess Maisy hesitated. Letty knew this was a signifi-cant request, but it was important to her. She was sure it would be better for the princess this way.

"You want me to abandon the plans I've been making?" the princess asked hesitantly.

"No, no, of course not," Letty assured her. "There's nothing wrong with trying to make things beautiful or helping the prince feel comfortable, and I'll keep helping you with that, too. I'm only saying that how you behave is more important than how you look."

Princess Maisy's eyebrows knit together, and the corners of her mouth drooped into a disappointed frown. "Letty," she said slowly. Letty smiled. It was the first time the princess had ever called her by name, which felt like a victory all on its own. "I want to, and I'm willing to try, but I'm not sure . . . I'm not sure I know how. It's been so long since I've really thought about how I treat people . . ."

"That's all right," Letty responded gently. "I'll help you as long as you promise to try."

After a few seconds of consideration, Princess Maisy nodded. "I promise."

Letty smiled, excited for what was unfolding. It felt like a brand-new opportunity. The princess seemed genuine when she said she wanted to change. And to be able to help Princess Maisy while also being able to visit her family—Letty could hardly imagine a better arrangement. "Then I'll stay."

Letty thought she saw something shift in the princess's eyes. Although they were usually ice-cold, there seemed to be a sudden warmth there.

"Thank you," she whispered. The princess turned to face Isla. "Guards," she said, "you may go back to your posts. You—Isla, was it?—are free to leave."

Jocelyn reached out to give Letty's hand a squeeze. "I'm

so glad you're staying," she said. "I would have missed you. What would I do without the extra excitement you bring?"

"I guess you don't have to find out," Letty laughed.

"Well, now that that's all sorted out, shall we finish getting ready for supper?" Princess Maisy asked.

"Yes, of course," Letty replied, "but once we're finished, could I please go visit my family?"

"Tonight?" The princess's eyebrows rose. "That's sooner than I expected. There are some things that need to get done tonight."

"Please, can I do them in the morning? I promise I will finish them as soon as I possibly can."

"What's so urgent that you have to visit tonight?" The question was not mean-spirited; the princess seemed genuinely curious about why Letty was so eager to go home.

"I miss my family terribly," Letty explained.

"I'm sure you do, but certainly this could wait for just a few more days, couldn't it? There's just so much to do around here, and on top of it all, I was hoping you would help me make things right with the seamstress and her assistant."

How could Letty make the princess understand how important this was? As far as Letty was concerned, nothing mattered so much just then as seeing her family. She felt tears prickling at the backs of her eyes—not of sadness, exactly, but of longing. "I haven't seen my mother in over a week. I spoke with my brother once through the window, and I haven't heard any news of my father since that visit."

"I see." Princess Maisy looked thoughtful. "What do you mean when you say you haven't heard news of your father? Is he traveling?"

"I hope so," Letty said. "He went missing about two weeks ago." One of the tears that had been building spilled over now, and Jocelyn, still silently observing the exchange, reached for her hand to comfort her. "There are search parties out looking for him, but they haven't had any success so far, at least from the last news I heard."

"Oh, Letty, I'm sorry," said Princess Maisy. "It's been a long time since I've missed someone like that, but—" Letty saw tears begin to pool in her eyes, too, and the princess swallowed hard before continuing. "If I try hard, I can remember. Not very much—I was very young when I lost my parents—but I do remember that missing them hurt terribly. I'm so sorry."

"Thank you," Letty said. "If I could just go visit later tonight, it would mean so much."

"You should go now," Princess Maisy said gently.

Letty's eyes widened. "Now? Really? But Your Highness—"

"Please," Princess Maisy interrupted. "I've kept you from them long enough when I shouldn't have. Go be with them. I'll manage for tonight. However, if it's convenient, I would like it if you could be back in time to help me get ready in the morning."

Letty stood awestruck. How different this felt from the

rest of her time with the princess!

A smile played at the corner of Princess Maisy's lips. "What?" she asked. "I'm practicing being considerate and respectful. That's what you wanted, isn't it?" Letty nodded, still not entirely sure she believed what she was hearing. Princess Maisy's gentle smile turned into a full laugh—the first Letty had heard from her since arriving at the castle. "Go ahead," Princess Maisy urged. "Fetch your shawl and go home. I'll see you in the morning."

Letty typically avoided running in the castle—it seemed inappropriate. She didn't think about that now, though. As soon as she was sure the princess was serious, Letty sprinted up the stairs and to her room faster than she could ever remember running. She located her shawl thrown over a chair, draped it over her shoulders, and was back in the grand entry in a minute flat. As Letty burst out of the giant front doors, a new sense of adventure settled over her, and with it came a sense of freedom. Whatever happened next was her choice, and she could feel in her bones that it would be exciting. All that could wait, though. Right now, it was time to see her family. With that thought, Letty took off running down Lantern Lane.